DREAMSPEAK 2

Alice I Blackwelder

Dreamspeak 2
Guide to the Symbolic Language of Dreams

Copyright © 2009 by Alice I Blackwelder

R.e.m.ember Your Dream Team is a branch of Eagles Nest Ministries
www.yourdreamteam.org

Eagles Nest Ministries
Randy & Alice Blackwelder
135 Malden Road
Mattydale, NY 13211
www.youreaglesnest.org

TABLE OF CONTENTS

Acknowledgments

Most of my life I've been aware of my dreams, spending time upon waking considering what they might mean. Some powerful dream experiences convinced me that there was some importance to them, and possibly a higher purpose in their being given to me, but my research on the topic led me to philosophies and symbol directories that made me sense a check in my spirit and left me feeling more confused than satisfied with the answers for my dreams.

It has been said, "When the student is ready the teacher will come." and in my experience it is true. I just didn't realize the extent of God's hand in getting the student ready as well as in providing the teaching.

I had a powerful dream within a dream that was repeated in its entirety two times. Each of the four segments seemed to end with my feeling that I was waking up and therefore thinking that in the next segment I was really awake. When I finally did wake up it took about twenty minutes for me to settle myself and understand that I was at last really awake. It was so powerful that I knew I had to understand what it meant. But even after sharing it with my pastor and some other trusted friends, I could not find anyone who could tell me what it meant, only that they agreed it was very important.

Not being a TV watcher, for some reason I was clicking through channels and came upon the Benny Hinn program. I had seen his crusades before and thoroughly enjoyed watching people give testimony but this show was different. Benny announced that he would be speaking with an expert in dream interpretation on the show that day, and proceeded to introduce and speak with John Paul Jackson of Streams Ministries, International. I was stunned and immediately realized that this was God's hand leading me to find the answers I had been seeking.

Within days I found out that John Paul Jackson would be coming into our area to hold a conference, so I immediately registered. During the conference, John Paul spoke of the classes he offered and his heart to instruct people in how to interpret dreams. I was ready, my teacher had come.

From the first class I felt that John Paul was a spiritual father and my heart was to learn all I could from him. I took every class that was offered and began work on the Web site *interpretmydream.com* which is devoted to training those who are called to interpret dreams. I read John Paul's books and listened to all of his teachings.

ii

There are not words to fully express how grateful I am to John Paul, a man who is always gracious, attentive, and willing to be transparent, even to the point of openly sharing his own mistakes. At a time when I was so desperately hungry for true spiritual meat, he was the one who provided the meal. When I felt near panic hearing the wonderful things he had experienced, he allayed my fears by helping me understand that my natural mind was simply struggling over its collision with the Spirit of the true and living God.

My journey has come full circle. Having experienced the desperation of desire for answers and having been provided with the necessary tools to find them for myself, I offer this guide to help those who, like me, may have no one else to ask.

I want to acknowledge that though the words written here are my own, I fully realize that each one bears an imprint of John Paul Jackson's wisdom and understanding and for the gift in my life that he is, I am thankful.

I also want to acknowledge the impact that Jim Driscoll of Interpretmydream.com and stirthewater.com has had on my growth as a believer and a dream interpreter. Without his careful mentoring, as well as his wonderful example, I would not have come this far.

There are many friends, my brothers and sisters, fellow followers of Jesus, who have helped in the process of sharpening me, and for all of you, I am thankful. Thank you to Lana Whisman who prophesied over me concerning writing and continued to occasionally remind me of that word. Lana, there is more to come.

Four wonderful women of God took the task of finding all my errors, of which there were many, and assisted in making this guide the best that it can be; thank you to true examples of representing God in the earth: Tipton Abrahams, Merry Bruton, Liz McGee, and Emilie Huxley.

Last but by no means least, I acknowledge the gift that I have in my wonderful husband, Randy, and my children, who, though many times they did not understand what I was experiencing or the depth of my "weirdness," continued to love, support, and encourage me to complete this work.

To each one who will read this, thank you for not giving up. It is my hope that your use of this resource will not only open up the meanings of your dreams to you, nor only help your ability to interpret dreams for others, but that it may release a greater hunger for communication with He Who Loves You Most. As you learn to recognize His voice and see His fingerprint in different areas of your life, may the world of communication with God in your dreams open before you a whole new realm of intimate fellowship with your Creator.

Introduction

What you have within these pages is considered a dream symbol dictionary, a compilation of dream symbols and their possible meanings. But I contend that it is more than that. The word dictionary is defined as follows:

Dic·tion·ar·y [**dik**-sh*uh*-ner-ee] –*noun, plural* –ar·ies. 1. A book containing a selection of the words of a language, usually arranged alphabetically, giving information about their meanings, pronunciations, etymologies, inflected forms, etc., expressed in either the same or another language; lexicon; glossary: a dictionary of English; a Japanese-English dictionary. 2. A book giving information on particular subjects or on a particular class of words, names, or facts, usually arranged alphabetically: a biographical dictionary; a dictionary of mathematics. Dictionary.com Unabridged (v 1.1) Based on the Random House Unabridged Dictionary, © Random House, Inc. 2006.

A more accurate description of what you now possess is simply a window into the world of ***dreamspeak***. It is a guide to the symbolic language of dreams. It is my firm conviction that God speaks to us through dreams. To fully understand what is being said, it is important to understand the language in which it is spoken. There is an Eastern proverb that says, "The great teacher is the one who turns our ears into eyes so that we can see the truth." While I do not consider myself a great teacher, it is my intent to put into your hands and heart the way by which you can see what is not there, hear what is not said, and understand the truth of what is presented.

God, the Great Creator, having His entire majestic palette at His disposal has chosen to speak to us in living, moving, breathing, action. You cannot read the ancient writings without noticing that the writers all participated in teaching eternal truth by means of stories that acted out in full and living color what they desired to convey.

Our English language is full of picturesque language that literally conveys a mental picture carrying the message of a thousand words. In our everyday language we speak in metaphors, similes, allegories, parables, etc., without giving much thought to the figure of speech used. Many of us probably don't realize how often we use these in our ordinary speaking, but understanding these figures of speech and how they work may be helpful in understanding the different ways dream messages can be conveyed.

A **metaphor** is the comparison of two seemingly unrelated elements. You simply take the first element and describe it as though it were the second. The word metaphor comes from Greek word *metaphora*, "a transfer" and *metaphero*, "to carry over, to transfer."

One example is to describe the circulatory system in a human being as though it were a highway system on which many cars travel. Another is to describe an automobile as though it were a human woman. It is quite common to hear men say, "she runs like a beauty," or to even give their vehicles female names.

In the English language, the use of metaphor is so profuse that I believe most people do not realize how much it is a part of our normal conversations. Thus, metaphors are also a very integral part of our thinking and help us to assign deeper meaning to what is said. By the use of metaphor, we can provide a broader scope of understanding to those who understand the "transfer" of one element's attributes or characteristics to another.

Many times in dreams, we see the use of one element and its story acted out before us, only to realize upon interpretation that the element is symbolic of something or someone entirely different.

A **simile** is the comparison of two subjects where their marked similarities are noted. You can tell a simile by the use of the words "like" or "as" or "than," or "resembles."

Examples of similes are phrases such as "she is as sharp as a tack" indicating someone's mental acuity; and "he walked through my life like a bull in a china shop" to describe the seemingly inconsiderate and damaging influence of a person who has been a part of your life. Dreaming of a bull doing much damage in your dining room may indicate just that.

A **parable** is usually a brief story that illustrates a moral or religious lesson. It is different from a fable in that fables use animals, plants, inanimate objects, and forces of nature as elements, while parables use human characters. A parable is like an extended metaphor but, unlike a simile, a parable's meaning can remain unspoken though it is not ordinarily hidden. With a little contemplation, the true meaning of the parable will be easily understood. The ancient writings give us many examples of the teachings of Jesus told in parable form. While the depth of the meaning may be lost to those of us who are strong Western Greek thinkers, the pictures painted by the stories Jesus shared would have been easily understood by those who were present. The struggle for most was the translation of the truth of the parable into the spiritual reality it represented.

The word **allegory** also comes from the Greek word *allos* which means *other* and the Greek work *agoreuein* which means *to speak in public* and is a figurative way of conveying a meaning rather than using literal expression. Allegories can be expressed through different media and not always in story fashion. *Allegory* is sometimes found expressed through realistic painting, sculpture, or some other form of representative art. Some popular allegories are C.S. Lewis's *Narnia Chronicles* and J.R.R. Tolkien's *Lord of the Rings Trilogy.*

Understanding the use of metaphors, similes, parables, and allegories will open your understanding of dreams by allowing you to see what is not there, hear what is not said, and understand the message that is presented.

It is such a part of our normal expression of language; I hope to help you see that simply looking at dreams using your eye for figures of speech can enable you to understand the message being conveyed.

The listing of words that follows is a compilation of terms that have been learned over years of study in dream interpretation. You will find simple nouns followed by what could be termed a definition; but understand, the definition is not what you might find in a regular dictionary, but rather what that particular word might mean in the context of a dream. You will also find phrases listed that are metaphors or similes with their natural meanings given, so with some listings the "definition" is the dreamspeak; and with others the actual entry is the dreamspeak. As you peruse the list you will see what I mean.

It should be noted that this list is always growing and is by no means exhaustive. It should also be understood that while it may be hard to comprehend, every symbol used in a dream has a possible positive or negative meaning. There are no absolutes, so if you read what is offered for a particular word and none of it seems to meet your criteria, then congratulate yourself. You have found what may become an addition to the guide!

You may want to take a particular entry and think of it in terms of the opposite of what is given. Just by having a starting place for contemplating a particular symbol, you can sometimes have a revelation of its meaning.

It should also be emphasized that since it is God who gives the message, it is He who has full understanding of what is being said. It is also He who releases understanding of the meaning to us by speaking to those whom we have asked to interpret our dream, or to our own hearts. But remember, it is God who interprets the dream.

I am of the opinion that not all dreams are to be interpreted. Dreaming is a natural phenomenon and many times we will experience dreams that are produced by our bodies for natural purposes. It is a scientific fact that all humans dream, most dream every night, and most dream multiple dreams every night. This process is essential for our mental health. Studies have shown that when humans are deprived of sleep for three nights consecutively, they will begin to show signs of a nervous breakdown. Dreams can be affected by illness, medications, or agitated mental state. There are dreams that are generated out of our own desires and/or fears that are called soul dreams. These are not to be considered messages from God, and though understanding their cause may benefit us, they carry no specific message for us to figure out. It is also my firm belief that over time, as you value your dreams and your communication with God, you will grow in your ability to tell the difference in the types of dreams you are experiencing and know which ones you should give your attention and energy to interpreting.

Included in this Guide you will also find meanings for colors, numbers, a brief introduction to the Hebrew "alephbet," the perils of religious language, types of dreams you may have, countries and their mottos, states with their nicknames and mottos, and Jewish prayers for preparation for sleep.

ARE DREAMS RELEVANT TODAY?

"Five things are a sixtieth of something else; fire, honey, Sabbath, sleep, and a dream. Fire is one-sixtieth part of Gehinnom. Honey is one-sixtieth part of manna. Sabbath is one-sixtieth part of the world to come. Sleep is one-sixtieth part of death. A dream is one-sixtieth part of prophecy."

Babylonian Talmud, Brakhot 57b

ARE DREAMS RELEVANT TODAY?

Have you ever tried to learn a new language? The older you are the harder it is, for as we age we lose some of our ability to memorize. We also lose our ability to think in new ways. I am sure you have heard the saying, "being set in one's ways". This really refers to having a certain mindset and how difficult it is to change our way of thinking.

Dreams have long been thought of in our culture as irrelevant images resulting from eating before bed, being under too much stress, or just a physical phenomenon that is required to keep a person from going insane. And while there may be some truth to some or all of these points, dreams are also a deeply spiritual phenomenon which many times can be a communication from God written in a language specifically created for you. We call this our dream vocabulary, or what I have penned as dreamspeak.

We are spiritual beings having a human experience. This experience is designed to prepare us for eternity. It is not designed to help us achieve only comfort in this realm. We are essentially in the school of relationship, developing our ability to communicate and get to know intimately One with whom many of us would say we want to spend eternity. The question is begged then, why would you want to spend forever with someone you don't even talk to or really know now?

Our dream life is a deeply personal time when all our defenses are down. Our rational thinking is disengaged to some extent and our spirit is open to another dimension. We can receive information about ourselves, others, and more specifically we can get to know God and grow in relationship with Him as we learn to listen and understand the messages He gives while we are asleep.

People of old have shared their dream experiences with us in the Ancient Writings of Scripture and I am sure you have dreams of your own that you know are of great significance. We are told in the Ancient Writings that even those who did not follow nor serve God received messages from Him in their dreams. As we read of the life of Joseph in Genesis we can see how God used a ruler's dream to bring Joseph out of prison and put him in a position to be used of God to preserve the nation of Israel. I have heard testimonies of people who have had their own lives preserved through instruction received in a dream.

You may say, "But that was then, and things are not like that in today's modern world." But I would say that God has told us clearly that He never changes. He is the same yesterday, today, (and therefore does the same things, acts the same way, and communicates the same way) and forever.

Or your response may be "That may be for some people, but it is not for me, I never dream." It has been scientifically proven that all people dream as many as 5 times each night. It is most likely that because of our culture you have conditioned yourself not to remember them, believing their message is of no value to you today.

I would challenge you to ask God to speak to you in your dreams and to help you remember them. I have a friend who did just that. Having told me that he never dreams, he accepted my challenge. That very night he had a vivid dream that he remembered and recorded. He received a wonderful message as to his life's call and a great encouragement in his relationship with his Creator just from asking.

You are never too old to learn a new language. It just may be harder now than when you were young, but it is not impossible. Make a deliberate effort to communicate with God before you go to sleep tonight and just see what happens.

HOW DO I PREPARE?

*We dealt much in soulfulness; we forgot the holiness of the body.
We neglected physical health and strength and we forgot that we
have holy flesh, no less than Holy Spirit ... Our teshuvah [return]
will succeed only if it will be – with all its splendid spirituality – also
a physical return, which produces healthy blood, healthy flesh,
mighty, solid bodies, a fiery spirit radiating over powerful muscles.
With the strength of holy flesh, the weakened soul will shine,
reminiscent of the physical resurrection.*

from Rav Avraham Yitzchak Kook, Orot (1920)

HOW DO I PREPARE?

So you have made the decision to go for it! Congratulations! A whole new wonderful world awaits you while you sleep. I want to discuss some of the ways that you can prepare to receive from God. It is important to prepare your heart as well as your physical surroundings so that you not only receive a good night's sleep, but that you receive all that God may say to you in the night.

Your bedroom should be a place of sanctuary where you can go and find not only rest, but peace. If that is not currently the case, you may want to make some changes. First, sit down in your room for a few minutes and take note of how you *feel*. Then take a look around. If there is a lot of clutter, things that do not belong in your room, move them. Straighten up any book shelves, clear off the top of that dresser that has stuff piled on it. Put things in their places making sure that all surfaces are not only clear of clutter but of dust, so that your room is actually physically clean, and then sit down again and see how it feels. I recommend continuing to clean out and organize until you can sit down and feel completely at peace in your "new sanctuary". Now that we have taken care of the physical surroundings, we can focus on the spiritual atmosphere of the room.

The Ancient Writings, which some call the Scriptures, or Holy Bible, tell us that those whose hearts are stayed on Him (God) will remain at peace. Peace is a wonderful thing that we all long for, though our definitions of what that actually is may be very different. It is essential to receiving not only a sound sleep in the natural, but is critical to receiving revelation in the spirit. That is why we are also told not to go to bed angry. Anger disturbs our ability to rest and gives dark forces of negative energy, sometimes called demons, an open door to harass us.

It is within the spirit of peace that revelation comes. And without peace, it is very difficult if not impossible to receive from God. Now don't despair, no matter how difficult things are for you right now, and how far away true peace may seem, God has promised that if you will just come to Him and lay down your burdens, He will give you peace. It may be helpful to visualize this action, or act it out. Take a piece of paper and write on it all the things that seem to be "weighing" on you, making you unable to feel completely at peace. Then symbolically lay them down at the feet of the One Who Loves You Most, Yeshua, known in English as Jesus, Anointed One of the Most High God. Yes, it really is that simple.

Once you have laid down all that troubles you, then ask God for His peace, which is called *shalom* in Hebrew and means quiet, contentment, rest, that is given to such a degree that you know it comes from God, not just from the absence of earthly troubles. Just ask Him for it, especially as you lie down to sleep.

You may want to add a ritual to your bedtime preparation. Most of us already have one, even if we don't call it that. We change into our sleep clothes, we wash our face, brush our teeth, use the potty, apply our night crème, etc. Most of these things simply prepare us physically to sleep. With the addition of a few simple actions, and the act of turning our attention to those actions before our time of sleep, we can prepare ourselves emotionally and spiritually.

As mentioned before, we must not go to bed when we are angry. After all, what is the point? You will only toss and turn and go over and over in your mind what made you angry and the things you should have said or done, or wished you had said or done. Then you will have a dream that is based on your bad experience and/or feelings and when you wake up you feel tired and cranky.

It may seem to be easier said than done, but you can make a decision to no longer be angry. It really is a choice. Forgiveness is a very powerful weapon that we all possess. It is simply a matter of choosing to wield it. You may find this prayer useful to recite until you feel that you can fashion your own words.

> *Great Creator/Heavenly Father, as an act of my will*
> *I choose to forgive all those who have done anything*
> *to or against me this day whether knowingly or*
> *unknowingly, by their words or actions. I choose to*
> *allow them to be free from any judgment that may*
> *result from their offense against me. I allow my*
> *forgiveness to freely flow toward them and release*
> *all anger so that it may fall to the ground powerless.*

Once you have released forgiveness you will want to welcome Holy Spirit and open your heart to communicate with God while you sleep. I like to take a moment to anoint myself with a dream oil God directed me to make. It is called Dreamwalking Oil, a mixture of pure olive oil and a special blend of organic essential oils. I like to take a few drops of oil on my fingertips and as I rub the oil on my temples, the sides and back of my neck, I recite a prayer similar to this:

Welcome Holy Spirit, I ask that you come and commune with me as I sleep. I love you, I thank you for Your Voice, help me to hear what You are saying and to understand all that You would show me.

The act of anointing yourself and praying a prayer of invitation not only changes the spiritual atmosphere of your room; it changes your perspective so that you see that your time of sleep is much more than one of natural refreshment. After I have anointed myself, I prefer to sit on my bed and pray the prayer of Invocation of Angels listed in the back of this book.

Another step you will want to take to prepare to hear from God is to put a pad of paper and a pen next to your bed. Upon rising, you will want to record all that you can remember from your dreams. Even if it is just a "snippet" of a scene or conversation, write it down. Even though you can't remember the whole thing exactly the way it happened, and everything that you saw and heard, it's okay; just write down what you do remember. You will find that over time you will remember more and more.

Should you be one who finds it difficult to write, you can purchase a small tape recorder to keep by your bed. When you wake up, hit the record button and tell the story as you experienced it. Later, you can take your time in transcribing your dream into written form. I encourage you to keep your dreams in a notebook or journal of some sort.

You may also find that playing soft instrumental music as you go to sleep will help you to come into a place of sweet peace that will enable you to sleep soundly. It is during the deepest sleep that we experience our dreams.

If possible, try to wake up before your alarm goes off, since being jarred awake will sometimes cause you to forget what you were dreaming. To make preparations to go to sleep may seem a little strange to you, but I can assure you, if you make the effort, God will meet you there.

18

KEEPING A
DREAM JOURNAL

Remember the Talmudic teaching that advises patience for dreamers:
"One should wait the fulfillment of a good dream for as much as twenty-two years."

Babylonian Talmud, Brakhot 55b

WHY KEEP A DREAM JOURNAL?

You may wonder why you should keep a dream journal. For some people it seems like just one more thing to do when they already have too much on their plate. To that I say, you give your self and your time to that which you value. If you truly desire to communicate with God in your dreams and begin to value them you will need to keep a record.

Remember the time that you heard a hilariously funny joke? You laughed until the tears ran down your cheeks and your sides ached. "I'll never forget that one!" was what you thought at the time. Not long after, at a lull in a dinner party you wanted to share the joke that you enjoyed so much; unfortunately you couldn't remember the three different elements that led so brilliantly to the punch line.

Our dreams can be powerful encounters with the unseen Creator of the Universe. Though we think we will never forget them, once our conscious mind is engaged upon waking, the images and details slowly slip away. Depth of feeling can dissipate as the "busy"ness of life demands our attention.

Journaling can be a powerful tool in the development of your relationship with God, but it is essential in the development of understanding your dream vocabulary. As you journal your dreams, over time you will notice a consistent use of certain images or people. Then you will notice a certain theme or pattern develop which will speak to you in a very specific way.

There are times that a dream may not make any sense now, but over time as you learn the way God speaks to you, that same dream will have a powerful message, a message that you will miss if you do not write down your dreams and review them regularly.

Writing can be a chore for many of us. But journaling does not have to just be writing. It can be drawing, sketching, word bubbles, in any fashion that helps you remember the dream experience and message. Don't be afraid to experiment and find the way of recording your dreams that works best for you.

You will be amazed after you compile a number of dreams and go back over them, how God will direct your life. In my own personal experience, I journaled my dreams before I understood them. When reviewing them, I realized God was giving me clear direction for specific circumstances at that time; however I did not know how to hear Him. Now I pay close attention to my dreams and am growing in my ability to hear His voice and follow His leading.

If God appeared in front of you right now and began talking to you, do you think you would write it down as soon as you could? You probably would not want to miss a single detail, but would want to note every inflection and choice of words so that you gain full benefit of the experience, and so you could share it with others at a later time. Many times a dream can be a visit from our Creator.

DEVELOPING A DREAM VOCABULARY

"…making your ear attentive to skillful and godly Wisdom, and inclining and directing your heart and mind to understanding – applying all your powers to the quest for it; yes, if you cry out for insight and raise your voice for understanding, if you seek Wisdom as silver, and search for skillful and godly Wisdom as for hid treasures; then you will understand the reverent and worshipful fear of the Lord and find the knowledge of our omniscient God."

Proverbs 2:2-5

DEVELOPING A DREAM VOCABULARY

Understanding of your dreams will come from the Spirit of God as He teaches you to hear His voice in the night season. Just as when you talk with someone close to you, you develop a vocabulary, so it is with your "dreamspeak".

By "dreamspeak" I mean that depth of communication that takes place between two people who are intimately related. When you talk with a close friend, or lover, there are instances when you try to relay what you feel in your heart. You can say so much, then only add, "You know what I mean?" and you know that they do.

This type of communication is developed over time. Dream vocabulary is developed this way as well. Your first step in learning what your dreams mean is to talk with the messenger. He desires for you to understand what He is saying. He will help you increase in comprehension and interpretation of what you see and hear in the night. Don't forget to ask Him.

Journaling is very important. It allows you to begin to see patterns in use of symbols, metaphors, etc. The thing that seems irrelevant at the moment of waking may be the central theme and you will not realize it until you look back over your journal entries.

Drawing can be a telling part of your dream. What seems to jump off the canvas of your mind may be the heart of the message. Upon waking, take a few moments to sketch what you saw. This is not art class. It does not have to be detailed, nor perfect. A stick man with a pipe may be all it takes to spark the mental rerun that enables you to remember the message given by the man with the pipe.

Jot down the conversations engaged in and take note of names that are spoken. There are many good books available and sites online that will enable you to understand the meaning of a name. I use the following rule of thumb in my own dream journaling: If a name is spoken out loud such as, "This is Anne.", or attention is specifically drawn to a person such as "Consider him," and I know the person's name then I treat the name as a piece of found treasure. It is to be examined and information on it obtained. This is also true of names of cities, states, countries, etc. When they are obviously indicated in a dream treat them as important.

Take note of color. Dreams are usually either black and white, normal every day color, muted color, or vivid living color that you have never seen in the natural. Color is a vital indicator of the depth of the message and the origin of the message.

Communication is key to developing a real and lasting relationship. I am not talking about prayer. I am talking about dialogue. You share your heart and you listen as your partner shares his/her heart. The same is true with God. He wants to share His heart with you. Take time to listen. Value His communication enough to write it down. Just as you value and meditate upon the Scriptures, realize that He is a living God who speaks today. Discuss what He has said with Him and you will grow in your love for Him and your understanding of His ways.

The Dreamspeak Guide

"For one who speaks in an unknown tongue speaks not to men but to God, for no one understands or catches his meaning, because in the Holy Spirit he utters secret truths and hidden things (not obvious to the understanding). But on the other hand, the one who prophecies – who interprets the divine will and purpose in inspired preaching and teaching – speaks to men for their upbuilding and constructive spiritual progress and encouragement and consolation."

I Corinthians 14: 2-3

Dreamspeak	Definition
Abacus	Reckoning; calculating; taking stock; visual rendering of accounting
Abandoned	Neglected; left behind; rejection; letting go
Abortion	Intentionally cut off; anything that does not reach full maturity; may indicate need for prayer against miscarriage
Abscess	Indicates some issue that is festering and needs to be expressed to obtain healing
Academy award	Accomplishment; reward; honor; outstanding performance
Accident	May be warning; consider what type of accident
Account	Explain your actions; place where your money is kept;
Acorn	Small beginning that leads to great things
Acrobat	One who is daring; someone who is strong and agile; going through difficulties to reach goal
Actions speak louder than words	No matter what you say, behavior says what you really believe
Actor / actress	May indicate someone playing a part; someone is not letting their true feelings be made known
Actor / actress (actual)	Consider who it is (real life or characters played) and how you feel about him or her; consider the meaning of his or her name
Adam	First man; one who first sinned; means earth; the first one; lack of duality; whole
Adrenals	Has to do with the fight or flight impulse; strength or lack of it; may indicate a decision that has to be made
Adultery	Divided heart; act of being unfaithful
Advertisement	Announcement; the word is out; seeking;
Affair	Unfaithful; secret association or alliance
Afghan	Type of blanket; warmth; security
Agate	Stone in the breastplate of the High Priest for the tribe of Benjamin; symbolizes ability to see in the spiritual realm; love for spiritual truth; banishes fears, healing for tender gums.
AIDS	Being destroyed from within; Messiah complex (some people feel compelled to "fix" things and people) that actually damages relationships
Air	Breath of life; may indicate speech; Great Spirit
Air balloon	Peaceful; riding the Spirit; increase when heat is increased
Air Force	Discipline; power; service of a high kind
Air-conditioning	Relief from the heat; one's breath or lung capacity
Airplane	Company; organization; the service or function you are destined for; group that moves in the Spirit; your spiritual journey; a trip; a message from above; spiritual journey that is taken with many others
Airplane – can't fly	Plans that never got off the ground; group not functioning in its life purpose
Airport	Place to be launched into your life purpose; getting ready to take off in the Spirit; may be a sign that you have paid the price for spiritual advancement (ticket)
Alabaster	Symbolic of extravagant worship; pouring out of self; deep meditation
Alarm clock	Wake up call; pay attention; timing; note time and define the numbers

Alcohol	A spiritual thirst quencher; a potential inclination to lose control; intoxication; a dehydrator
Alien	Stranger; foreign; out of character; unfamiliar
Alley	Narrow pathway or road; usually closed in or hidden
Alley – right up your alley	That is in your area of expertise
Alligator	Lies in wait to catch its prey; controlling attitude; exerting influence; large and powerful mouth; tough exterior; obnoxiously aggressive; gossip
Almanac	Information for the future; intercessory instruction
Almonds	Resurrection; spiritual awakening
Altar	Offering; selflessness; purification; associated with whatever we worship
Ambulance	Vehicle that brings help in emergency situation; ability to usher in healing and restoration; a way has been made
Amethyst	Purple (see "Colors"); stone in the breastplate of the High Priest for the tribe of Dan; believed to provide protection, spiritual attunement, to give visions, reduce mental tension, induce pleasant healing dreams, prevent overindulgence and encourage transformation and breaking of bad habits
Amphitheater	A place where things are magnified; usually open air
Amputation	Abandoned talents and serious, permanent loss
Amulet	Good luck charm; protection; superstition
Anchor	Stabilizing factor; being tied down; hope
Anchor – taking up	Willing to change or move out into something new
Ancient	Wisdom; age; rare; valuable
Angel	Spiritual messenger; ministering flames of fire; spirituality; heavenly protector
Animals	Transparent spiritual issues; consider the characteristics of the animal as well as color; consider your feelings toward the animal
Animation	Humor and comedy in most situations
Ankles	Faith; vulnerable to being tripped up; strength of spiritual walk
Answering Machine / Voice Mail	Equipped to get the message; ability to hear in the spirit realm
Ant(s)	Industrious; wisdom; preparation for future things; pest; uninvited or unwanted guest(s); social conformity and mass action
Antiques	Good or evil inherited from ancestors; memories; things from past; ancient ways; items that usually come at a high cost
Antlers	Authority; strength; weapons of war
Anvil	Instrument of fashioning; place of being beaten down in order to be shaped
Apartment	Not permanent; transitioning; seasonal; usually refers to a timeframe of six months to a year
Apocalypse	End times; may indicate need for prayer for intervention; warning of drastic change or coming turmoil
Apple of eye	Most cherished person; someone who is closely protected

Apples	Sin; temptation; fruit of Spirit; fragrance; sweetness; beauty, peace; wisdom; prosperity; health
Apron	Symbolizes protection, secrecy, readiness to work
Aquamarine	Blue-Green (see "Colors"); believed to give direction in one's life; lift one's spirits; provide protection at sea
Aquarium	You may feel that your life is going nowhere; you feel you are going in circles; feeling of being confined; life seems on display
Arcade	Joy; amusement; escape from reality; playing games that have a cost to them
Archer	Messenger; one taking aim, taking a particular course of action
Arena	Look at context; could indicate competition; may indicate exposure to large audience
Argument	May indicate an offense, unforgiveness, an issue that has been suppressed but not dealt with; feelings that need to be expressed
Ark	Place of safety in the spiritual realm; Jesus in humanity and deity
Arm	Strength; might; faith; look at which side is accentuated (right-authority; left-destiny); victory; power; talent or aptitude
Armadillo	Seems to be clothed in armor; may seem to be a formidable foe; nuisance, harasser, destroyer
Armies	Power and strength; good or evil
Armor	Divine equipment for warfare; grace; may indicate a tough exterior
Armored car	See "Car – armored"
Arms	Weapons
Army	Giving up your own will; discipline; may mean large number
Aroma	Fragrance; awareness of presence; worship
Arrested	Issues of control and restraint
Arrows	Specific word of God to you personally; children; the Word; lies and deceit; bitter words; silent judgments; gossip; overcome by love; particular course of action; tool to reach a goal
Art Gallery	Works of art on display; in position to gain new perspective
Arthritis	Condition that affects the joints causing pain; indication of anger, bitterness that have been allowed to remain
Artichoke	Heart of some matter
Artist	Creative expression; generally refers to one who creates; may also indicate someone who is covering up, an illusionist
Ashes	Repentance; destruction; total death of old life; memories consumed; mourning; shame; humility
Ashtray	Place where remains are placed; indicates lack of value, no substance
Asp	False teacher; venomous lie(s)
Asparagus	Prosperous times; poisonous if consumed consistently over long periods
Asthma	Something hinders breath; may indicate a spiritual condition that keeps Spirit from moving
Astral Projection	Out of body travel; denotes acting by one's own will
Astronaut	One who travels in the heavens; person who is prepared to go high in the Spirit

Athlete(s)	Competitor; discipline; faithfulness; teamwork
Atlas	Book of maps; compilation of information concerning direction; knowledge pertaining to travel
Atom bomb	Extreme power to bring radical change; sign of the end of the world; sign of Jesus returning to earth; sudden destruction
Atrium	Glass has to do with vision, light, and growth from heaven
Atrium with plants	Plants imply growth; right atmosphere for growth; protected environment
Attic	Family history or past issues; place of storage; things which are forgotten or neglected; usually dusty indicating neglect; old things; valuables; memories; ways of thinking
Attorney	Advocate for justice; one who pleads your case before a judge; Jesus; someone who prays for others or for divine intervention in a situation (also called an intercessor)
ATV (all terrain vehicle)	Vehicle that moves easily across rough terrain; ability to navigate through many types of circumstances; type of life purpose or work done for others that be dangerous if not handled carefully
Auction	Determination of worth; those who are willing to pay the price get the item
Audience	May indicate you are in a situation where you are being watched, inspected with intent to judge your abilities, etc.
Audition	Opportunity to show your talent; seeking approval of others
Aura	Energy field that is evident around all living things; color of aura indicates meaning (see "Colors")
Aurora	Dawn; coming of light; Aurora Borealis—a display of heavenly light
Author	One who gives birth to written creation
Auto repair shop	Renewal and restoration of some aspect of your life
Autograph	Has to do with fame or importance; being recognized or sought after; speaks of your identity; Consider the person named
Automobile	Speaks of your self, your work, or your current situation in life; you will want to look at the different parts, etc. metaphorically (Example: steering wheel won't work = things in your life are out of your control; speeding = need to slow down)
Autopsy	Procedure to obtain information that cannot be readily seen; feeling torn apart; determination of root cause of death; may provide intercessory information
Autumn	Repentance; change, completion
Avalanche	When things seem to come crashing down on you; seems there is no escape
Awakening	Generally refers to a spiritual revelation rather than just waking up; if experienced while dreaming indicates you may begin to experience lucid dreaming
Awaking	Resurrection; preparation; revelation
Axe	Tool used for chopping or splitting apart; may indicate abuse; extreme anger; preaching; exhorting; rebuke; judgment; destruction; pride; is sometimes two-edged

Baby	Work done for others or responsibility; new fresh thing happening; those who are new at learning about spiritual things; a gift; multiplication of the same kind
Back	Courage; strength; support; lower back may indicate support issue
Back adjustment	Bringing things into proper alignment; aligning courage
Back – direction	Past; past experience; backsliding
Back porch	Family history; past issues; place of quiet reflection
Badger	Badger someone; someone who is aggressive, easily irritated
Bag – In the bag	Assured of a successful outcome
Bag – lady	Someone who has been abandoned, rejected; making use of all resources
Bag – Trash	That which needs to be disposed
Bag / Baggage	That which one uses to carry belongings, purchases, etc.; shows that you are carrying stuff around
Baggage – excess	Indicates personal problems; issues that haven't been dealt with
Bait	Consider the type: may indicate some type of temptation, trap
Baker	Those who prepare the spiritual bread to give to others, freshness of God
Bald head	Having no wisdom; having no covering; anointing; mourning (Amos 8:10); may indicate maturity
Bald tires	Lacking the proper foundation and/or direction to go forward safely
Ball	Consider the type: may indicate wholeness, completeness
Ball – dropping	May indicate someone is not doing their part
Ballpark figure	To get an idea of the approximate cost of something
Ballroom	Roomy place to dance and/or worship; large room; typically elegant requiring particular clothing to enter
Banana	Gentleness, kindness, goodness, soft-hearted (also, bananas are 'a-peeling' wordplay for appealing); glory, vitamins essential to the heart
Bank	Heavenly account; favor or usury; place of exchange; stores favor
Banker	Ability to give favor or offer opportunity for people; one from whom you may seek favor or provision
Banner	Identifying flag; something that is better than expected; help; love; majesty; standard
Baptism	Prophetic act that makes declaration of new spiritual birth; purification ceremony; being totally consumed by something
Bar Mitzvah (boys) Bat Mitzvah (girls)	Ceremony to mark becoming a son or daughter of the commands; indicates time that a young person takes on the responsibility for his or her own spirituality
Bar, such as pub	Place where spirits are served; gathering place for those looking for something spiritual; in a negative sense, may speak of "looking for love"; wanting escape
Barbed Wire	Fencing material; may indicate an offense; painful
Barber shop	Change in customs, habits, traditions
Barbie Doll	Society's norm for young girls; speaks of perfection that is desired or despised; unrealistic expectations
Bare feet	See "Feet"

Barn	Place for storing food; place of dispersal; where animals are housed and protected from elements; Kingdom of the Great Creator
Barrenness	Unproductive; death of spirit; death of what you feel is your life's purpose; unable to bear fruit
Basement	Lowest level of house; core beliefs; foundational issues; things hidden or stored; things unseen that affect spiritual life; flooding; forgotten; carnal nature; soul; lust; depression
Basement – cracked walls	Indicates weakness or previously unseen problems in one's foundational thinking or beliefs
Basket	Tool used to carry supplies, may indicate ideas, resources; if full indicates provision; if empty indicates lack or that time has not come yet; may also refer to the womb
Bat(s)	Night flyer; may indicate some occult torment; believed to bite for blood; devourer of pests; operate by sonar (akin to discernment) someone who uses spiritual perception; nocturnal; doesn't like light; can ruin harvest
Bathing	Cleansing; regret for past actions; temptation; purification; preparation
Bathroom	Place of privacy; dealing with spiritual repentance; time of confession; cleansing; being purified; getting rid of toxins, time of receiving relief from things troubling you
Bathroom – Go in front yard	Purification will happen in a way that is noticed by others; or may speak of a time coming in the future
Bathroom – playing	With excrement: making light of what you need to get rid of
Battery(ies)	People; getting energized by something; refreshing of power
Battle	Spiritual warfare and/or revival; conflict
Battlefield	Geographic location of a battle; memorial; scene of skirmishes
Beach	Sands of time; mass of people; to be in a position where you can't move; place of relaxation and/or exploration
Bear – positive	Courage to stand and fight; word play for bare; person (usually male) who is large in physical size but has a gentle heart; person who is protective of those he or she loves; depth of loving nurture of a mother; strength
Bear – negative	Exposure of whatever is bothering you; can indicate a demonic force or evil person that is dangerous to you; supplanting authority; financial downturn; people who pretend to be compassionate but are scheming and conniving; sudden explosive power; danger; implies death; bears will stalk; rage; something that attacks; word play for bare; judgment
Beard	Maturity; strength; honor; age; covering; notice if it is neatly trimmed or messy
Beauty shop	Preparation; vanity; place where you undergo transformation; time of purification
Beaver	Ambition and hard work
Bed	Place of rest; place of intimacy; sexual sin; laziness; ungodliness; situation you have chosen (made your bed)
Bed & breakfast	Temporary intimacy; provision of time of rest and nourishment; same as hotel
Bedroom	Rest; privacy; peace; covenant (good or bad) intimacy; slumbering; laziness

Bee(s)	Producer of honey; one who knows how to work in a group; delivers a painful sting; those who bring about fruitfulness; busy bodies; gossip; group of people; enemy invasion; can indicate attack of negative spiritual forces
Bells	Indicator of time; expression of joy; angelic activity; calling
Belly	Symbol of emotional extremes; love/hate, desire/lust, selfishness, self-worship; may refer to appetite; mercy; time of uncertainty
Belt	Truth; readiness
Beryl	Emerald and Aquamarine (see individual gems); represents moderation; control of passions
Bicycle	Life purpose or work done individually for others; gifting, work; requires self-effort to propel along; working alone; something you are trying to do by yourself
Bier(s)	See coffin; punishment; false teaching; state of apathy; foretelling of death
Big banana	Boss (not polite); a derogatory way of looking at authority
Big butt	May indicate a person is lazy or has become apathetic; improper distribution of tasks
Big toe	Walking in great authority; out of balance in a big way
Bikini	Minimum covering
Billboard	Sign that is seen by many; announcement
Bind / bound	Close relationship; oath; marriage; unity; addiction; something that is destined; a hindrance
Binoculars	Ability to see clearly at a great distance
Birdcage	Feeling of being trapped; false sense of security; limitation
Birdhouse	Place of nurturing; protection
Birds	Consider color, behavior, type (characteristics); God; Great Spirit; Satan; angels; being snared; escape; pride; swiftness; some type of spiritual being (good or bad)
Birds –devouring	Dark birds indicate an evil spirit; negative thoughts or forces that cause you to doubt what you believed before
Birth	Resurrection; restoration; bringing forth what may seem impossible; something new
Birthday Cake	Celebration; usually marks important time
Birthmark	Usually a dark or red mark on the skin; may represent being marked for a purpose
Bite the apple	Sexual intimacy outside of marriage; give in to temptation
Black	See "Colors" section for expanded definition
Black – in the black	Out of financial danger
Black ball or list	A list of people or organizations that are boycotted or punished in some way
Black belt	In karate, it identifies a highly-skilled person; may indicate a person who may be dangerous in certain situations
Black magic	Wicked, occult, witchcraft, voodoo; using spiritual power for negative reasons
Black – blackmail	To try to gain what you want by making a threat, usually to divulge information that a person wants kept private or secret

Black market	Illegal trading of goods or money
Black out	Period of loss of electricity or power; period of loss of consciousness
Black panther	Evil force that stealthily approaches and/or attacks; someone who operates at a high level of evil; rebellion
Black sheep	An outcast; usually the family member that gets into the most trouble
Black tie event	An event that is formal and requires formal attire or training
Black Widow	Poisonous spider said to kill its mate; warning of danger regarding relationship
Black-hearted	Wicked person; someone who has impure motives
Bleachers	Position as spectator of a competition; may indicate feelings of helplessness, that you can only watch what is happening and can't do anything about it
Bleeding	Spiritually dying; wounded; hurt emotionally or naturally; strife; gossip
Blemish	Imperfections of human nature; defilements; false teachers
Blimp	Heavenly; powered by the Great Spirit; doesn't progress quickly
Blind	Lost; without understanding; self-righteous; lack of discernment; unlearned; religious spirit; false teacher; pride
Blister	Indicates something that has been "rubbing" you the wrong way; painful experience; anger (as in blistering mad)
Blizzard	Snow storm that causes inability to see
Blood	Life; covenant; murder; unclean; witness; guilt; life of flesh; grace; vengeance
Blue	See "Colors" for expanded definition
Blue – (emotion)	Sad; feeling depressed
Blue – blue ribbon	First prize
Blue – into the blue	Going to unknown heights
Blue – out of blue	Something you were not expecting
Blue – ribbon panel	Group of highly-qualified people
Blue – true blue	Loyal and faithful
Blue birds	Communion and favor; happiness
Blue garment	Spirit of revelation, might and power
Blue in the face	To be at your wits' end; feeling that you are not being heard
Blue Jay(s)	Revelatory gifted people who use revelation from others as though it were their own; mockers; announce the rain is coming
Blue skies	Happiness is coming; things are getting ready to change
Blueberries	Nutritious fruit that indicates abundance; provision; revelation; may also indicate receiving information for intercession (prayer for divine intervention offered for others)
Blueprint	Details of foundational issues
Blues (singing)	Sad songs; indicates a type of mourning and/or lamenting of life or a particular situation

Blurry	Unclear vision; may indicate that you do not have a clear picture of a situation
Boat / ship	Group or organization that is powered by Great Spirit; swiftness of life; wife who is faithful
Boat / ship Ocean liner	Large movement or group that focuses on helping others
Boat / ship Sailboat	Powered by the wind, or Great Spirit
Boat / ship Speedboat	Fast moving, short-lived, exciting
Bobcat	Wild cat; aggressive; stalker; powerful earth-mover machine
Body odor	Unclean spirit; filthiness of flesh; rejected
Bomb	Warfare; instrument of destruction; may indicate a sudden expansion;
Bones	Spiritual condition of heart; death; eternal; structural support (consider condition)
Boogie board	Used to ride waves; indicates equipped to move in spirit realm
Book (by the book)	According to certain rules
Bookkeeper	One who manages finances; may speak of person who knows the score, understands all the details of a situation
Books	Can indicate man's knowledge; knowledge of God; preparation for this time; Word; learning; divine revelation; Wisdom; knowledge; education; record
Bookshelf	See Library
Bookworm	Person who likes to read a lot; may indicate someone who lives in fantasy; strong intellect
Boomerang	Indicates that whatever you throw out to others will ultimately be what comes back in your own life (some people use the term karma)
Border crossing	Overcoming barriers; making a transition; calling into a different country
Boss	May speak of your literal boss or someone who has authority in your life, i.e., pastor, husband, head of committee, etc.
Bottom dweller	Scavenger, freeloader; someone lacking discernment
Boulders	Obstacles; difficult to navigate
Bow	Power of God in your life; might of a nation; verbal attack; accusations; slander; prayer; deliverance; judgment
Bowling	Consider how you feel about the sport; may indicate you are attempting to knock down an opponent; skillful intercession
Boxes	Unused, unopened gifts
Boxing	Close contact sport; may indicate you are fighting with some issue
Boy	Those young in faith; literal relative; neighbor
Boy Scout	One who is properly trained and prepared for every situation
Bra	That which gives support to those who are nurturers
Bracelet	Wrist adornment; consider type, color, gems, any message
Braces	Support; stronghold; that which gives guidance to your understanding
Braids	Neat and orderly thinking; restriction; legalism

Brakes	May indicate a slowing down that is needed; forward progression being hindered
Branch(es)	Believers; rejection; Messiah; judgment; certain group; victory; rejoicing; churches or sects; God's people; relationships, growth, new life
Brass	See "Colors" section for expanded definitions
Bread	Words in Bible; voice of God; crushing; kneading; staff of life; doctrine; covenant; provision; Jesus; group of followers of Jesus; discipline; vanity; truth; idleness
Bread – fresh	Revelation of the moment; prophetic; coming directly from the throne of God
Bread – moldy	Old sermons; no direct revelation; tradition; stale; defiled; carnal interpretation of Word
Breakdown	Total loss of self control; inability to handle process
Breakfast	Early morning meal; may represent time with God; breaking of a fast
Breaking	Slow down, brake, take a break
Breast feeding	Careful nurturing of young; bonding; teaching
Breasts	Nurturing; caring for young; God is known as the many breasted one (meaning of the Hebrew name for God *El-Shaddai*); one who gives comfort to those who are weak
Breath	Life; creative power; brevity of life; death
Brick	Building block; can be used in a destructive manner; strength
Bride	People who believe Jesus is Messiah; covenant; Israel; one who enters a covenant with another
Bridegroom	One who enters a covenant with another; Jesus
Bridges	Faith; (if broken, little faith); support; joined; transition; crossing over into something new
Bridle	Used to rein in an animal; give direction
Bright light	Indicates that it is God
Broken heart	Suffered a type of deep hurt
Broom	Cleaning; put sin away; witchcraft; to sweep away
Brother(s)	Literal family members; members of your fellowship; those in your sphere of influence
Brown	See "Colors" section for expanded definitions
Bruises	Friendly counsel; sign of a previous wounding; damage that has been below the surface
Brush	Instrument for untangling thoughts; warning of brushing things off; consider the type, color and condition
Bubble	Place of protection and bliss; joy
Bubble bath	Relaxation in the Spirit
Buckler	Someone or something that protects us
Buffalo	Intimidation; complete provision; strength; survival. herd means tranquility, plenty
Bug	Something bugging you (may be an insect or a VW brand vehicle called a bug)
Builders	Family; leaders; obedience; spiritual growth

Building 7–11 store	Convenience; place to purchase quick, non-nutritious food; may want to consider the meanings of the numbers
Building(s)	Under construction; take note of size, condition, type of building
Bulb	New life; new idea
Bull(s)	Leaders; enemies
Bulldozer	Large transition; moving; destruction; pushy personality
Bumblebees	Indicates power to overcome the impossible
Burden	Responsibility; suffering; guilt
Burial	Connected with death; may indicate being in over your head; overwhelmed
Bus(es)	May indicate you are "getting" somewhere; usually has to do with traveling to a place of learning with a group; traveling that has a cost; being taken by someone else; similar to "Car", but is larger and hold more
Bus – Greyhound	Same as "Bus", but larger impact
Bus – School bus	May indicate a destiny of teaching others
Bush	Fullness of spirituality
Butter	Smooth speech; insincere motive; the best; anointing
Butterfly	Symbol of transformation; freedom; eternal life; resurrection; indicates having been through a lot that results in beauty
Buttons	Fasteners; pay attention to color and what article of clothing is being buttoned; wordplay: to button up means to keep quiet
Cafeteria	Lots of choices for spiritual nourishment; could be a seeker-sensitive church; could indicate desire for more choices
Cake	Celebration; something you desire
Cake – and eat it	To have things turn out much better than you expected; to get exactly what you wanted
Cake – icing on	The best part of a situation or person, etc., that seems to surpass all expectations
Cake – piece of	Meaning that something was extremely easy
Cake – that takes	Usually indicates exasperation; may indicate acknowledgment of something good
Calves	Joy
Camel	Endurance; carries burdens or is to go into intercession; goes long distance and time without water; known for hump (burden being carried); hypocrisy; impossibility; lusting after sin
Camera	May indicate your need to focus to gain greater understanding; ability to capture a moment, remember, recall an event
Camp	Time of "roughing" it; vacation; temporary living conditions; enjoying freedom
Camp – in the same	Means to be in agreement
Camp – outside	Disgrace; separation; isolation
Can	Word play "you can"
Cancer	May indicate being destroyed from within

Candle	The light that we give off; comparisons to someone or something else (i.e., that doesn't hold a candle to…)
Candlestick	Light bearer; Jesus; those who make up the group of followers of Jesus (also called the Church)
Candy	Something that seems sweet but is not good for you in the long run; temptation; reward
Canoe	Impact; influence; self propelled; solo
Cap gun	Noise but no power
Cape	Mantle; authority; consider color and condition
Captain	Headship; leadership; Jesus
Car	Refers to your personal life; such as your job, your physical body; your personal life purpose or may refer to your church/fellowship; carries more people, has covering, costs more to own, operate, and maintain
Car – armored	Protected; usually only used when transporting money (favor, provision) what you do for others or a vocation that is surrounded by strength; possessing great protection
Car – convertible	Open heaven; revelation; clear thinking; as you move about you have open access; surety of answered prayers
Car – jeep	Being totally exposed; able to be adventurous; able to travel off the beaten path
Car – limo	Call of God; formal; expensive; usually reserved for special events; consider color; sign of importance of the rider
Car – parked	Life purpose, spiritual life or job on the sidelines, doesn't seem to be going anywhere; things in your life seem to be at a standstill; usually temporary; may indicate a time of rest
Car – repair	Receiving some type of healing in your life and/or life purpose
Car – streetcar	Local church or fellowship group; that which carries people along in life; may indicate a particular group of people
Car – taxicab	Hireling; a means of moving forward in your spiritual journey with a cost to it; may be a warning of being taken for a ride, which will cost you
Car as female	She runs like a dream; isn't she a beauty
Car crash	Conflict; could entail two or more groups or personalities that are not getting along
Car runs like a dream	Car operates as it is supposed to or better than expected
Cards – he's a card	Means that someone is a jokester or funny
Cards – house of	Means things are precarious; unstable conditions
Cards – playing	Dealing with what is going on in your life
Carnelian	Stone in the breastplate of the High Priest for tribe of Reuben; gives a feeling of well-being
Carnival	Entertainment; diversions; consider activity: riding rides may indicate you are being cheated; playing games of chance may indicate you are taking a gamble
Carpenter	Jesus; one who builds or repairs

Carpet	Foundational covering; subservience; comfort
Cart	Judgment; blessing
Casino	Taking a risk; being wasteful; temptation
Castle	Fortress; authority; glory; royalty; city of God; stoicism; unchanging; soulish imagination; fairy tale; hierarchal issues
Cat	Depends on how you feel about them; usually considered aloof, not affectionate; can represent a watcher spirit; independent thinker; gracefulness; speed, strategy; slinking; treachery, ambush; will or willfulness; issue of the soul
Cat – black	Usually indicates something coming that is not good
Cat – out of the bag	Means to divulge information
Cat's Eye (Gem)	Helps heal the eyes; helps one see their own faults; understanding; able to see in the dark
Cathedral	Older environment; place of worship; grandiose;
Cattle	People; groups of people who seem to follow
Cave	Place of hiddenness; time of deep prayer on behalf of others when you are not at liberty to discuss things; potential solemnity or focused concentration on God; dark night of the soul
Cedar	Spiritual renewal; King David of the Bible; repels moths, may indicate protection from irritants that would eat away at your abilities
Ceiling	Covering; protection; limit; ways of thinking
Ceiling – hit the	Reach your limit; lose temper
Cell phone	Same as telephone; mode of communication that is personal; may indicate receiving information (such as intuition); may represent prayer; your need to contact someone
Centaur	Witchcraft; head and trunk of a man, body of a horse; may indicate someone struggling with their own spirituality
CEO	God; one with great authority; head person
Chaff	Insignificance
Chain link fence	Boundaries
Chains	Discipline; punishment; bondage; used to pull; connection
Chair	Rest; position; concentration; receiving; authority; to have obtained goal; finished work; consider color and condition
Chakra	The word chakra means circle or ball. They are considered the 7 energy centers in the body which correspond to certain endocrine glands; may give off color which indicates health condition; said to be the connecting point of soul to body; frequencies correlate to musical scale; also called aura, outshining, emanation
Chakra 1 – Base	Red; located at the base of spine; correlates to musical note C; symbolizes being grounded; stillness
Chakra 2 – Sacral	Orange; located just beneath the navel and related to sexual and reproductive capacity; musical note D; symbolizes sexuality, reproduction

Chakra 3 – Solar Plexus	Yellow-gold; located at the solar plexus; seat of the emotions; Musical note E; symbolizes emotions and/or will power
Chakra 4 – Heart	Green; location correlates to thymus; musical note F; symbolizes love, compassion
Chakra 5 – Throat	Bright blue; connected to communication and/or speech; musical note G; symbolizes creativity
Chakra 6 – Third Eye/Brow	Indigo or white; located deep in brain; correlates to pineal gland; said to allow spiritual vision; musical note A; symbolizes intuition; imagination; revelator
Chakra 7 – Crown	Violet or White; located at top of head; correlates to pituitary; musical note B; represents spiritual understanding
Chameleon	Changes with its surroundings; someone who is not consistent; double-minded person
Champion	One who triumphs
Chariot	Something you will accomplish; expect an encounter with angelic beings; God's might; false confidence
Chased	Through house: something you need to deal with that you do not want to face; feeling that you can't handle your current situation
Cheek	Testing; suffering when smitten; forgiveness; enticement; temptation
Cheek – cheeky	Rude or speaking inappropriately
Cheek – tongue in	Not sincere in what is being said
Chicken	Scared or frightened person; non-flying bird; being afraid; may indicate a fear that needs to be dealt with; may indicate putting yourself in danger (playing chicken); may indicate someone who is controlled (henpecked); popular source of nourishment; used in promoting health (chicken soup)
Child	Reward; heritage
Childhood things	Past issues; consider timing
Children	Next generation; plants; arrows; heritage; reward
Choking	Too much too fast; hatred; hindrance
Christmas	New birth; spiritual gifts; benevolence; celebration of the birth of Jesus; generally symbolizes love, family, receiving of gifts; memories; pagan tradition; commercialism
Churning	Anger that has been brewing for a while; creating
Cigarettes	Wrong kind of spirit; addiction; commonality; being puffed up
Cigars	Celebratory; communing with others; exclusivity; conspicuous consumption
Circle	Endless; timeless; eternity; perfection
Circle of life	The life cycle of birth to death
Circumcision	Covenantal relationship; spiritual change; entering covenant; cutting away of flesh
Cistern	Faithful love; hidden spiritual supply
Cities	Circumstances in your life; actual city;
Citrine (gem)	Stone in the breastplate of the High Priest for the tribe of Naphtali; believed to provide cheerfulness, control over one's emotions, clear thought, and help to overcome mental blocks

City	Work of man; group of people dedicated to help each other; community
City – inner	God's inner city; inner city work
Clam	Closed off emotionally; cold
Clam up	Close one's mouth and refuse to talk
Clap (hands)	Joy; prophetic act toward victory
Clapping	Warfare; praise; exultation; rejoicing
Clay	Person; weakness; yieldedness; indicates ability to be molded, flexible; willing
Cleaning up	Taking care of messes; putting things in order; may indicate someone who is giving more time to "busyness" than to meditative practices
Cloak	Calling; zeal; mantle; authority; consider color and condition; hidden
Clock	Take note of actual time shown (see Numbers); may indicate time to do something; time running out; too late; too early; delay; your heart (ticker)
Clogged shower	Past things to be taken of
Closet	Hidden or secret sin; private; personal; prayer; aloneness; place of storage (memories, fears, etc.)
Cloth	Anointing; covering; what you are gifted to do
Clothing	Joy; strength; humility; compassion; covering; anointing; consider colors and condition
Clothing – wrong	You know you have something to do but are not ready to do it; wrong timing
Clouds	Bringing spring rain; favor; passing: one's welfare; invading army; God's glory; groups of people; blessings coming, Lord comes; truth obscured; trouble coming
Clouds dark	Indicate their source is dark; can be warning of depression or storm coming
Clouds white	Indicate their source is God; though a time may be rough to go through you are assured it is for a good purpose
Clown	Not taking things seriously; playing with God; one who likes to make others laugh
Club	God's wrath; weapon used to beat; association of people for a common purpose
Coals	Shame; holiness
Coast	Border between two realms;
Coat	Mantle; protection; insulation; covering; if clean shows righteousness; may speak of what type of persona you show to others; consider color and condition
Cobra	Spirit of control and manipulation; won't back down; aggressive
Cobwebs	Indicate neglect; dusty; may indicate lies, deception
Cock	See "rooster"
Cockroaches	Same as rats, sneak in through cracks; eat off things that haven't been cleaned up; run from light; indication of underlying or hidden problem
Coconut	Hard nut to crack; once broken offers milk and meat
Coffee	Indicates need to be alert; consider your own feelings toward coffee, i.e. find it refreshing, relaxing, use it for energy, have an addiction to it

Coffin	Death; transformation; great change coming; end of situation; state of being unable to function
Coins	Usually represent people; may represent value, state, favor; consider denomination, condition, and time minted if shown
College	Higher degree of learning; training to walk in a higher dimension
Collision	Consider what type of vehicles are involved; cars are more personal; planes indicate spiritual group such as church or fellowship; ships speak of large organizations; typically being shown disaster of some kind is for the purpose of praying to change it
Columns	Foundational beliefs that support someone's thinking
Comb	Used to set things in order; removes snarls; provide a part (make a way)
Competitive place	Place of conquering
Computer	May indicate quick intellect; provide for quick exchange; source of information; source of communication; consider your feelings towards computers
Conception	Moment of new life beginning; to first have an idea
Concrete	Solid; firm; reliable; truth
Contacts	Man's effort to help you see; ability to see without source of vision being apparent
Controlled flying	Shows a level of spiritual self control that indicates maturity
Convertible	See "Car – convertible"
Cooking	Providing nourishment; applying heat to that which is to be understood; testing spirits
Coral (gem)	Aids in keeping control of thoughts while meditating and visualizing; helps heal arthritis
Cord(s)	To bind or be bound; that which connects; sin; death; affliction; bond of friendship
Corn	Provision; bountiful harvest; spiritual hearing
Corndog	A wiener or type of sausage link cooked in a batter of corn bread; meaty substance that is concealed in some other teaching; parable
Cornerstone	That with which everything else is aligned; Jesus
Corny	Something that is silly
Couch	Rest; too relaxed; lazy; unconcerned; usually refers to furniture in an informal room
Couch potato	A person who sits on the couch, watches TV, and eats junk food; a lazy person; sedentary lifestyle; person who lacks ambition; someone who has lost hope
Counter	A division; encounter (in counter); count you in; count on you
Country store	Serene; healing; place of provision; typically refers to a time in the past
Court	Exclusion from inner place; tribulation period; trial; time of testing in a relationship; place where justice is rendered
Covered wagon	Tradition; pioneering
Covering	Purpose, call; those who have spiritual authority in your life

Cow	A change coming that will take time and a lot of effort; provision; Word (milk and meat); overweight person; famine
Crab	Harsh personality; not easy to please; hard to get to know; can have to do with a painful relationship; in a bad mood; easily irritated; bad temper
Crabapple	Bitter person; fruit that looks good to eat but is actually bitter
Crane (bird)	Deeper things coming; machine used for heavy demolition or industrial construction; lifts a heavy load to extraordinary heights
Cream	Richness; anointing; fat (in a good way)
Creation	Artistic ability; creativity; beginning
Credit Card	When you are so sure of something you are willing to put yourself at risk for it
Crocodile – positive	People who have great power in their mouths and what they say has a bite to it; people who use their mouth for God
Crocodile – negative	Someone who is a big mouth; someone or something that can drag you down causing great harm; painful verbal attack; faker
Crooked	Twisted, distorted spiritually
Crops	Has to do with seasons of life and can indicate lengths of time; consider the type and the time of year, i.e., ready to be harvested; dying from lack of water; or newly planted
Cross	Usually symbolizes the cross that Jesus was crucified on; sacrifice; strength; spiritual victory; going through a difficult period; a burden
Cross the bridge when you come to it	Face a situation when it happens; may indicate naïveté, or failure to plan ahead
Crossing street	Having a change in your perspective; moving to a new location
Crown	Rule; reign; promotion; glory; honor; power; rewards; very top of the head
Crows	Mockers; laughers; death; plans of the enemy
Crucible	Purification; time of suffering; time of testing and strengthening
Crystals	Are conductors of gamma energy; may indicate deep truth; clarity; hidden beauty
Cuckoo	Crazy; type of clock that sounds the time with the sound of a bird
Cultural clothes	May indicate your need to pray for the nation depicted; may represent a cultural belief; may indicate heritage in the dreamer's bloodline; may indicate a destiny or passion connected to the geographical area or the people represented
Cup	Life; health; evil or good; can represent a duty; higher purpose
Cut and dried	Things are very basic, leaving no questions
Cut or bruise	Shaping you; evidence of wounding
Cymbals	Vibration; praise; worship; noise; lack of love; warning
Daily bear your cross	Deal with your own issues on a regular basis
Dam	Restriction of power; block; obstacle; source of great power; control of great power
Dancing	Worship; spiritual sacrifice; joy; rejoice; whirling; idolatry; seduction

Darkness	Ignorance; blindness; sorrow; distress
Dart	Sharp digs, usually by words; some type of painful experience; curses, piercing words, chants, or incantations; indicate attack of the enemy; may indicate accuracy
Dates	Consider the actual dates given (see "Numbers")
Daughter	Child of God; someone or something within your sphere of authority or influence; mentoree; literal daughter
Dawn	New day; morning; receive revelation
Dead body	Being dead in the gifts; may indicate a hidden issue that has come to the surface; may represent something coming to an end
Deaf	Inattentiveness; physically or spiritually unaware
Death	Final; end; termination; traditional religion
Debt	Something you owe
Decay	Rottenness; sign that life has ceased
Deceased	Seeing a person in a dream that is deceased is not to be feared. It is not uncommon for God to allow a person to return for some divine purpose. We are forbidden to call the dead to us, but Scripture gives us several examples of those who had died, appearing and communicating with those still alive.
Décor	Note the time period and consider the history of that time; also consider colors (see Colors)
Decrease	Less impact; regression in your spiritual growth
Deer	Passion for God; healing; heart; may indicate money (buck or dough)
Déjà vu	You've entered a time that you dreamed about but don't remember dreaming it; you've been prepared; something sealed in your spirit being revealed to you
Delivery	Receiving a gift or something you paid for; receive the equipping you need; may indicate a need for deliverance or actually being delivered of something
Deposit	Payment that assures your gaining possession at a later time
Desert	Desolation; temptation; wilderness; time of trial; dark night of soul
Desk	Place of learning or preparation; where work is done; bills are paid
Devour	Completely consume something; eat very quickly
Devour a book	Read very quickly
Dew	Refreshing; usually comes in the early morning or late evening
Diamond	Clear for clarity, can be yellow (see "Colors"); believed to help heal respiratory problems, and provide attunement to higher forces; believed to open the crown chakra; resolve, hardness; clear revelation, hearing clearly
Dice	Taking a gamble; playing with chance rather than making a decision
Dining room	Sanctuary; place of fellowship; where you partake of spiritual food; family meeting place; where decisions are made
Dinosaur	Something outdated; very old person or thing; old issues, perhaps stemming from past generations
Diploma	Acknowledgement of accomplishment

Dirt	Earth; gossip; consider condition: rich dirt provides health to plants
Disease	Something that attempts to destroy health
Dishes	Your ideas, beliefs; what you are working on; how someone is treating others (what they dish out) or how they are being treated.
Dive bomb	Attack
Diving into a problem	Giving all your energy to find a solution
Divorce	Breaking of an agreement; dissolution of a covenant; destruction of a marriage; painful
Doctor	Jesus; healing; recovery; restoration; one who heals
Dodo	Derogatory term for someone who is considered dumb or foolish
Dog	Can indicate a friend; watchdog; conscience; faithfulness; unbeliever; one who bites; intimidates; bad man; ugly woman; consider the breed and its traits; meaning depends on context and your own feelings about them
Dog eat dog world	People will take advantage of you if they have opportunity
Dog one's trail	Follow a person intently
Dog-eared pages	Pages that show wear or have a corner folded down; a reminder
Dolphin	One who travels easily in spiritual realm; playful; spiritual communication; has no fear of man; talkative; show-off
Don't bite off more than you can chew.	Don't agree to or try to do more than you can accomplish.
Donkey	Strength; burden bearer; gentle strength; democrat; stubborn; someone who is an ass
Door	Your heart; new opportunity; portal; place of transfer from one realm to another
Door – Back	Refers to issues in the past; leads to time of relaxation
Door – closing	Making a choice; opportunity no longer available
Door – Front	Refers to future; more formal entrance
Door – Open	Opportunity available; usually involved a decision whether to go through or not
Door – Trap	Indicates surprise opportunity; potentially dangerous
Doorway	Threshold; opening in a wall
Double – dream	Very important; life call; exclamation point; destiny; is going to happen
Double number	Doubling of whatever the number means
Dough	Money; revelation (as it is the foundation of bread making); teaching that is still being formulated in your mind
Dove	The breath of God; wings = place of rest, protection, favor, love
Dragon	Usually stands for the enemy or his plans; wordplay as something is "dragging on" longer than expected; magical; mysterious; someone whose words are powerful, i.e., fire breather
Dragonfly	Strong positive spiritual force or aspect; Native American symbol of a Seer; bravery
Dreadlocks	Usually associated with false religion (reggae); or rebellious person

Dream	To commune with God while asleep; to see in the spirit realm and desire to possess or realize what is seen
Dreamers	Visionaries; those who have hopes
Drift	To lack direction; to get off track
Drinking	Taking in spiritual refreshment
Driving in reverse	Moving in the opposite direction from which you should be headed
Dross	That which is not valuable, made apparent by heat and pressure
Drowning	To have more to do than you can accomplish; desperation; totally immersed in the spiritual realm; it is not unusual to dream that you are drowning only to find that if you relax, you are able to breathe under water
Drum	Sounding an alarm; your own life's direction; your beliefs; raising support
Drunk	Under the influence of some type of spirit
Duck	One of the unclean animals; indicates a false doctrine or teaching that is off (a quack) avoiding an issue; being in a bad position (a "sitting duck"); stick your head down like a duck fishing in a pond or lake.
Dung	That which is of no worth; refuse
Dust	Earthly minded; thinking that hasn't changed in a long time
Dusty	Indicates something has been left sitting for a long time; gifting that has been neglected; something lost
Dwarf or midget	Someone who may seem insignificant; something that has not grown properly; sometimes used in literature for mischievous creatures
Dying	Transition; time of great change or shift; something coming to an end
Eagle	Soaring in the Spirit; good or evil leader; strength; sharp vision; stays above the chaos; a destiny involving revelatory or prophetic gifts
Eagles	Prophets; those who move in the revelatory gifts
Ear	Hearing in the Spirit; lack of hearing; pay attention
Ear muffs	Used to keep ears warm; may make hearing difficult; can be preferable not to hear
Ear muffs – red	Wisdom in hearing; something that is keeping you from hearing
Ear of corn	See "corn"
Earring	An adornment for the ears; that which draws attention to the ears
Ears	Someone who pays attention to what is going on; spiritual hearing; good listener
Earthquake	Judgment; shaking of beliefs; testing of faith; caused by God; upheaval; change by crisis
East	Sunrise, light; God's glory arising; birth; birth; new day; things changing; imminent
East wind	Mercy
Eat your heart out	Really want something that you can't have
Eating	Taking in spiritual food; partaking of what is offered; getting nourishment
Ebbing away	Progressive movement away from beginning point; something that is weakening

Echo	Repetition; gossip; accusation; mocking
Eden	Paradise; place of communion with God; fullness of provision
Egg	Fragile; seed; promise; plan; potential; revelation; life
Egypt	Bondage; slavery; tremendous scientific advancements; ancient; ruled by pharaohs
Eighteen-wheeler	Large vehicle usually used to bring goods; indicates blessing and/or provision; consider the number (see "Numbers")
Elbow	Joint; joins two parts; connects relationship; allows movement of arm (see "Arm")
Electricity	Power in the Spirit; source of information or insight; demonic
Elephant	Someone or something that has a great impact, power to accomplish; wisdom; strength; never forgets; force; something that has been designed to attack your mind; humanistic thinking; memories; religious spirit, return to old things; good luck (in some cultures); someone who is thick skinned; demonic force; may indicate an issue you have been ignoring (the elephant in the room)
Elevator	Indicates spiritual progression or a change in the level of anointing you have; going up indicates increase; going down indicates decrease; make note of floor number and use definition of number for further insight
Emerald	Stone in the breastplate of the High Priest for the tribe of Levi; green (see Colors); meditation; healing; business success; it totally rejects evil; believed to give power to foretell future events; a link with spiritual forces; kindness; goodness
Emotions	Consider what you feel in the environment or atmosphere of the dream; emotions can be a good indicator of the truth; consider what is felt while experiencing a dream, not after waking and logically thinking about it.
Engagement	Promise; meeting; to enter in to some type of event or conversation; the first step to making a deeper commitment or entering into a covenant
Engraving	Permanently marking something; mark made by grinding or digging out material used; may indicate experience of great pain that has left a powerful impression; indelible impression
Envelope	Usually used with the receipt of a message; communication; may indicate a new idea
Eraser	May indicate need to let go of something; removes evidence of error
Escalator	Spiritual progress without self effort; consider direction
Escalator – no rails	No boundaries
Evaluate	Make a decision as to something's worth
Evening gown	Moving in an anointing of great price; you paid a high price for what you are clothed in
Exodus	Moving out into a whole new realm
Explosion	Sudden expansion or increase in good or evil; swift change; destruction
Eye	To watch; to see; ability to understand; desire for good or evil; covetousness; passion; lust; revelation; insight

Eyeglasses	Enhanced ability to see; something that helps your understanding, gives clarity
Eyelashes	Long: visionary with discernment
Eyes – coming out	Vision or ability to see has been given up or stolen; eyes coming out of hand: one function trying to operate in another function;
Eyes – dilated	Trying to see more than you are gifted to see
Eyes – red	Demonic
Eyes – winking	Flirting with sin; deceitfulness; cunning; hiding true desire
Eyes – closed	Slumbering; refusing to see; unbelief; willing ignorance
Eyetooth	Element of understanding that involves spiritual vision or revelation
Face	Character; likeness; identity
Face – darkened	May indicate a force of the enemy
Face – lightened	May indicate an angelic being or someone who has spent time with God
Factory	Place of service, production
Fail safe	A sure thing; no worry of failure
Family pictures	Indicate family line; generation issues; may simply point to literal family members
Family tree	Your family lineage
Famine	Lack of hearing the Word of God
Fangs	Sharp teeth that deliver poison; may indicate cutting words; usually associated with anger
Farm	A place of provision and hard work; harvest or producing spiritual food
Fast	Moving quickly without a lot of effort; refraining from food, etc.
Father	God; wisdom; may represent your earthly father or someone who has played a positive role in your spiritual development
Feathers	Speak of a source of comfort and protection; may indicate an accomplishment; consider what type of bird they are from
Feet	Walk in spirit; ways; thoughts; conduct; formal possession; stubborn when still; Lack of peace, need more protection; in grass may indicate connection with creation; heart
Feet barefoot	Without preparation; without salvation; easily offended; tender
Feet diseased	Offense; some issue is affecting your walk
Feet kicking	May indicate rebellion; fighting against enemy; battling by using your character
Feet lame	Spirit of unbelief
Fence	Protection; enclosure; restraint; safety; tradition; boundaries; barrier; may indicate an offense; being unable to make a decision; something that has been stolen and then sold
Field	World; earth; God's work; harvest; opportunity; mixed multitude
Fig tree and/or figs	Israel; people of Israel; thought of as fruit, it is actually the flower of the fig tree; it is a false fruit where the flowers and seeds grow together in a single mass; provides shade; indicates prosperity
Fighting	Warfare; engaging in a struggle to be free from an issue
Fingernails	Indicate health (depending on their condition) and/or person's own efforts; can be used as a knife (see knife)

Fingers	Have to do with one's ability to relate to others; speak of direction if pointing; relationship when they are intertwined
Fingers – Index	Prophetic gifting; shows direction, points the way, is discerning
Fingers – Little	Teacher gifting; smallest finger easily fits into places such as your ears; the teacher opens up truth to the hearer
Fingers – Middle	Evangelistic gift; reaches out beyond the other fingers or gifts to touch lives; gathers in
Fingers – Ring	Pastoral gifting; covenants, relationships, compassion, emotional health
Fire	Roaring can mean wickedness; purification; trial; judgment of God; testing; Great Spirit; tongues (as of fire); time of feeling the heat; terminate employment of someone usually for a reason that is not good
First name	There are many references available to provide the meaning of a name; not all names in a dream are important; if attention is given to the name, then pay attention to it; otherwise disregard it; check meanings on behindthename.com or babynames.com
Fish	People; clean and unclean people; Something that doesn't seem right (fishy)
Fish – drink like a	Someone who consumes too much alcohol
Fish – eating	Indicates partaking of spiritual truth
Fish – fish for info	Trying to get information; trying to find out something without coming right out and asking
Fish – out of water	Someone who is out of their area of expertise
Fish – types	Consider their characteristics, habitat, color, how you feel about them
Fish tank	Exposure; containment; limits; limited scope of influence; limited ability to move in spiritual things; feeling of being confined or watched; place of safety
Fisherman	Someone who has a desire to help other people find their way to God;
Fishing	Helping people spiritually; trying to get information
Fishing boat	Indicates a group or organization whose focus is to help people in their spiritual journey
Flash	A sudden realization or insight such as the "light went on"; also speaks of something happening quickly
Flashlight	Personal knowledge or understanding; guidance; limited insight into what lies ahead
Flies	Lies; live off dead stuff; carry disease; may indicate negative activity
Flint	Solid; determination; provides friction to produce fire
Flock	Group of people; to be drawn to a particular place
Flood	Waves: my iniquities have gone over my head; judgment on sin; deluge; overcome; overwhelm; depression; large movement of the Spirit of God
Floodgates	That which is designed to hold water back or to control its dispersion
Flowered garment	Fragrant anointing

Flowers	Indicate an area or gifting that will bloom or come to fruit as you grow in it; give off a fragrance; may indicate grace; fading glory of mankind; glory; temporary; gift; romance; person who is a late bloomer
Flowers lily	Death; funeral; mourning; beauty; splendor
Flowers rose	Love; courtship; romance; Jesus and his followers
Flute	Obedient follower; musical instrument which requires wind (spiritual harmony)
Flying	Growing in spiritual realm; sign of maturity and advancing to new levels; ability to get over our circumstances; a destiny to operate in the revelatory gifts
Flying controlled	Spiritual maturity increasing
Foe	Enemy; negative power one has over you
Fog	Confusion; clouded issues or thoughts; obscurity; uncertainty
Food	Look at type and its effect on body; relate its attributes to what is being fed
Food for thought	Something to think about
Foot	Peace of God; no foot = no peace; your walk
Foot of the mountains	Area at the base of a mountain just where it begins to ascend
Footstool	Sign of complete rest; where you rest your feet
Forehead	Thought; reason; mind; memory; imagination; determination
Foreigner	Not of the flock; someone to view with care
Forest	Group of leaders; protected by leaders; the solution to a problem; place of contemplation
Fork	Indicates choice is necessary; utensil for eating; utensil used to make sure meat is done
Former place	Season you are currently in or coming to
Fortress	Place of protection; strong walled environment
Foundation	Dealing with foundational issues; your core beliefs; your thoughts; the lens through which you look at everything
Fox	Beautiful woman; cunning, crafty, secret sin
Fragrance	See "Aroma"
Freezer	Something lying dormant that needs to be refreshed; a place of storage for future use
Frog	One of the ten plagues; can indicate witchcraft; easily fooled; unclean; not one to speak up; person who can be fooled; lust
Front	Future; now; in the presence of; a prophecy of future event; immediate; current
Front porch	Vision; may speak of something that is to come; place to gather and fellowship; relax
Fruit	The outcome of your accomplishment; reward; proof of what has been sown; ripe fruit can signify something that is about to perish
Fuel	Power source
Full swing	Completely engaged

Fur coat	Mantle of prestige; gifting
Furnace	Heat source; heart; wrath; zeal; anger; trial; testing
Gall	Nerve; bitterness of temper; manifest by sores
Garage	Restoration; repair; rest
Garden	Indicates provision; where things grow; intimacy; romantic spot such as in Song of Solomon; place of hard work to obtain harvest
Garland	Fragrant adornment; intercession;
Garment	See "Cloth" or "Clothing"; consider type, color, condition
Garnet	Stone in the breastplate of the High Priest for tribe of Judah; deep red (see Colors) believed to aid in remembering dreams, for going backwards in time, attracting love, gives persistence, cures depression, works on liver to relieve toxins in the body; may indicate healing of bitterness
Gas station	Where you go to get refilled; a place of release of power
Gas station – Old	Outdated teachings; people who do not want to break with tradition; those who prefer to continue doing things the same way because that way is comfortable and familiar
Gasoline	Fuel; prayer; danger if there are fumes; poisonous doctrine
Gate	Entrance; power; authority; thanksgiving; entering the presence of God
General store	Serene, healing, soothing; place that offers a wide variety of merchandise
General – military	Authority; five-fold ministry spoken of in the Bible that includes those who function in the capacity of apostle, prophet, evangelist, pastor, teacher
Get under your skin	Something is irritating to you at a deeper level
Gift shop	Giver of gifts
Giraffe	The giraffe represents spirituality such as seeing far from a height, gentleness, long neck symbolizes willing spirit; people who stick their neck out for you; high things; able to give oversight; pride; high-minded; higher perspective
Giraffe – baby	Spiritual offspring or a new beginning.
Girdle	Strength for battle; a belt
Glass	Speaks of vision; usually clear; means tranquility in God's presence
Glass – broken	Tranquility disturbed, accusations
Glass – in mouth	Cutting words spoken by person with glass in mouth
Glasses (eye)	See "Eyeglasses"
Glove	Covering; protection; safe; careful; notice color
Glue	Signifies a sticky situation; something that is difficult to get free from
Gnat	Small irritation
Go home – kick dog	Relieve one's stress or anger, by hurting an innocent party
Goads	Instrument of compulsion; usually used to poke in provocation
Goat(s)	Stubbornness; one who gets the blame; blessing, abundance, stubbornness, carnal, flesh, will swallow anything: no discernment
Gold	See "Colors" section for expanded definition

Goldfish	Signifies valuable person; may speak of wisdom; friendship
Gorilla	Forcing something to happen; intimidation; strength; may indicate a pushy person who acts out of emotion rather than thinking things through
Graduate	Accomplish the task; passed the test; something that is over, completed
Grain	Faith; something that starts out small and grows; great potential
Grandparents	Heritage; bloodline; may indicate literal family members; depending on how you feel about your own grandparents: may indicate loving, nurturing, or spoiling
Granite	Doesn't break easily
Grapefruit	Self-control; sometimes difficult to endure self control but the fruit of it is sweet; control in the realm of the emotions
Grapes	Faithfulness; fruit of promise; loyalty, promises fulfilled; love slaves of God; friendship with God; depicts saying no to the world; good character; promise; wrath; Word of God; fruit of vine
Grass	New life; green
Grass – dried	Death; repentance; spiritual drought
Grass– if mowing	Crucifying the flesh; putting your life in order
Grass – mowed	Chastisement; sickness; financial distress or need
Grasshopper	Feelings of inadequacy; devourer of harvest; one who is blown by the wind, unstable
Grave	Indicates something that has died, i.e. ideas, dreams, hopes; hidden
Gravel road	God's way and the Word
Graveyard / grave	Hidden; out of past; curse; evil inheritance; hypocrisy; death; demon; major transition; gateway to new form of life
Gray	See "Colors" section for expanded definition
Gray hair	Maturity; wisdom
Grayed-out color	Indicates that there has been a weakening or may indicate that this is not of God
Green	See "Colors" section for expanded definition
Green around gills	Being sickly and pale; not able to receive spiritually
Green light	It is safe to go forward
Green thumb	Good at growing plants
Green with envy	Filled with envy
Green-eyed monster	Someone who is filled with jealousy; the spirit that provokes jealousy
Greenhorn	Someone who is not sophisticated; newbie
Greenhouse	Place of nurturing; survival not based on outward conditions; growing in an environment designed to produce success, but may not be "the real world"
Greenie	Newbie; novice
Greens	Leafy vegetables; may refer to currency
Grizzly	Particularly dangerous type of bear (See "bears"); situation that is extreme, serious

Grocery	Pick up provision, church; spiritual food
Ground	Your current circumstance
Gum	Chewing on things that can't be digested; doctrine that can't be swallowed
Gun	Power to reach beyond; what you are equipped with (depends on caliber, type, etc.); authority in the spirit realm (can be positive or negative); consider your skill with it
Gymnasium	Usually a place that requires discipline and hard work; place of training; may indicate being seen by many
Gypsy	One who is typically portrayed as dealing with the occult; good fortune; wanderer; someone who has not established roots
Hair	Covering; anointing; wisdom; strength; can have to do with identity, looks
Hair Long – man	Strength; defiance; rebellion; consider your own attitude toward men with long hair
Hair – long	Growing in wisdom
Hair – short	Wisdom has been affected
Hair on teeth	Australian slang term for indicating maturity; having endured something that caused you to grow up, become stronger
Haircut	Removing or breaking covenants or religious tradition; fixing up; getting things in order; new identity
Ham	A show-off
Hammer	Force; Word of God; preaching; evil words; destructive; to pound at something
Hamster	Feeling like you are not getting anywhere; working hard and making no progress
Hand	Your decision to let God move; your response to His ability; consider which hand (left or right); fellowship; relationship; assisting; applauding; five-fold ministry spoken of in the Bible that includes those who function in the capacity of apostle, prophet, evangelist, pastor, teacher; direction; also see "Fingers"
Handcuffs	Bondage affecting relationships; may indicate feeling that your hands are tied in a certain situation; prisoner; vulnerable
Handshake	Agreement; joining into relationship
Handwriting	Indicates being aware of what is coming; consider what is written, style, legibility
Hang by neck	Indicates someone or something that has been hindered or "hung up"; death; punishment
Hang glider	Moved by wind; humility; home group
Hanukkah	Jewish festival of dedication; time when Jesus declared he was the light of the world; also called Festival of Lights; usually occurs close to time Christians celebrate Christmas
Hanukkiah	Candelabra used during Hanukkah that has nine lamps or candles, eight for the eight days of oil supplied by God and one called the *shamash*, or servant that used to light all others.
Harlot	Idolater; adulteress; the church committing spiritual adultery
Harness	Used to give direction; indicates being in control

Harp	If used for God, a symbol of praise, worship; if used for the devil, lust, self satisfaction
Harvest	Reward of hard work
Hat	Covering; protection; thought; attitude; activities
Hat(s) – off	Indicates respect or congratulations
Hat – pass the hat	Indicates financial need; need of favor
Hat – thrown in ring	Decision to participate in something
Hawk	Speaks of extreme awareness and spiritual vision; counterfeit of eagle; psychic; one that preys on others; a cunning person; to sell something is said to "hawk" it
Hazel	Consider the meaning of name; eye color that usually is a mixture of more than one color; see Colors
Hazel tree	Beautiful flower and fruit; can grow almost anywhere; resistant to disease; bark & leaves used for medicine; sedative; brings comfort for pain; very hardy; resilient
Head	Speaks of who is in charge; may refer to mental capacity or lack of it; someone's intelligence; your belief system; the source or origin; elderly, honored man
Head – pops off	Intellect or stronghold pulled down
Head of lettuce	Measure of favor; mental acuity with finances
Head of the church	One who has authority over the rest; usually refers to Jesus
Healing	Being made whole; coming into a state of cooperation
Hearing	Tuning your spiritual self to listen; getting the message
Heart	Speaks of depth of emotion; love; core of your being
Heart of a lion	Brave
Heart of stone	Someone unable to express emotions; seemingly unable to love
Heel	Power to crush; weakness shows if you are not careful you can be taken down; may indicate the past
Heifer	Sacrifice; provision
Helicopter	Small group of people or cell group; very mobile and quick; gets in the spirit quickly and doesn't require a lot of preparation; rescue mission
Helmet	Salvation; protection to the head
Hens	Mothering, nurturing
He's a rat	Snitch or tattletale
Hidden room	Secret place; additional room (for getaway or for expansion) at your disposal that you are not aware of
High rise	Reveals your obtained spiritual height or level; shows a higher level in the spirit
High rise with a new roof	Great call but covering will be changed; change in thinking of a person or group; coming into a new revelation or level of understanding
Highway	Christian faith; way of life; choosing to do what is right; way of error

Hill(s)	Moving to a higher level spiritually; a small rise; midway point
Hippopotamus	Prophetic (its mouth is a prominent feature; eats and stomps down weeds so water does not become stagnant) they eat human beings; throw weight around and don't care who gets hurt; may cause one to think of Hippocratic oath, which speaks of healing
Hips	Loins; mind; truth; joint; offense between brothers; reproduction; stubbornness
Hit the nail on head	Made the point exactly
Hog	Greedy person; immoral; huge; noisy; gluttonous
Holding photo	Gaining a different perspective; memories; capturing a moment
Hole in clothes	Shows that your area of gifting has been neglected or been injured; may indicate a need to study your gift
Homing pigeon	Bringing a message home
Honey	Sweetness of spiritual relationship; promises being realized; Word of God; preservative; healing of wounds
Hook	That which grabs your attention; temptation; bait; make a connection
Hornet	Indicates an attacker, painful sting; aggressive; attack by dark spiritual forces
Horns	Strength; call to attention; call to prayer; call to action; announcement; alarm; music
Horns (animal)	Strength; authority; weapon of defense; abundance
Horse	Indicates power, may represent something God is doing; strength; philosophy or emotions to ride upon; pride in fleshly strength; authority; color is important
Horseradish	Used in Passover meal to represent bitterness of slavery
Hospital	Place of healing
Hot air balloon	Going into the heavenlies by the wind of God
Hotdog	Show off
Hotel	Temporary; where people stay for a time and then move on
House	This is where you live; usually shows that issue is about you or some aspect of your life; may also mean your fellowship (spiritual family)
House – inside	Inside: what's going on in your life, etc
House – Raining inside	God is moving in whatever room is represented, i.e. your bedroom means there are spiritual things happening in your intimacy with God
House – small	Speaks of the person that the house belongs to; if you are in an unfamiliar small house it may be speaking of areas in your own heart of which you are unaware
House – snow inside	Coming favor; neglect; heart has grown cold
House – trailer	Temporary place, situation, or relationship
House – upstairs	Going higher in the Spirit; of the Spirit; upper room; Pentecost; one's thoughts
House – childhood	Past, old issues, something there you need to discover or deal with
House – large	Group you are a part of such as your family, church, club, or work

House – living in someone else's	May indicate you have a similar gifting as they; also may mean you are not operating where you should or you have a desire for what does not belong to you
House – log	Historical past
House – new	New birth; change for the better; new move, either spiritual or natural; revival
House – old	Old man; past; inheritance; old ways
House – two story	Multilevel situation; spirit and flesh of a person, organization, double anointing
Hummingbird	Prophetic promises of fruitfulness; they only stay around a house that is pleasant
Hunter	One who is searching; may indicate a group working together; one who delights in the search; usually indicates respect for nature
Hurricane	Strong winds; destruction; positive: brings lots of water
Husband	Jesus or God; Satan; actual husband; pastor; boss
Hut	Temporary dwelling; usually indicates lack of structural strength
I took a shot at it	Indicates attempting to do something while feeling unsure of your ability
I'm dog-tired	I'm really tired; indicates a deep level of weariness
Ice cream	Reminder that God is good; God is bringing sweet things into your life
Idolatry	Worship of false gods
Immobilization of body parts	Usually in a spiritual warfare dream; shows you are under attack or are lacking in the authority to ward off the attack
In the red	In financial danger
Incense	Prayer; intercession; praise and worship
Incisor teeth	Indicates ability to decipher what things mean; (tear them apart); may also speak of your decision making
Index finger	See "Finger – index"
Information age	Time where information is easily obtained
Inheritance	That which is passed down to you from previous generations; may be good or bad; can include spiritual gifts, money, land, characteristics, misfortune, poverty, etc.
Inheritance – lost	Generally used to denote the loss of something good that was to be passed on to you
In-laws	May indicate legalism; actual relatives
Instrument	Instrumental; consider type of instrument, its condition, sound
Insurance	Faith; protection; safe; future provision
Intercessors	Those who are called to bear a burden before God on behalf of someone else. When interpreting dreams for them it is good to encourage them. Say something like "God gave you this dream because He trusts you; many struggle with the burden they bear.
Intimacy	About worship and close relationship with the Lord; or if lacking reveals lack of worship and relationship; may also speak of literal relationships
Invited	Called; a way has been made; favor
Iron	Great strength but will be corroded by water if not properly cared for
Iron and steel	Strength; power; strongholds; stubborn; affliction

Ironing	Correction; instruction in righteousness; pressure from trials; working out problems
Island	Stability, stable position; surrounded by water
Israel	Actually Israel; having power with God and man; chosen by God
It is raining cats and dogs	Raining in great amount of water that seem to fall at once; may manifest in a dream as being overrun with lots of animals; may indicate a great outpouring of God's Spirit, or His favor
Jade	Peace, tranquility; healing for eyes, believed to aid in going backwards in time, wisdom, universal attunement, said to give long life and a peaceful death
Jasper (Gem)	Stone in the breastplate of the High Priest for tribe of Asher; in wall of New Jerusalem; improves one's sense of smell, strengthens the desire to do good; helps to balance the emotions; satisfaction
Jaw	Strength
Jet	Church or large corporation
Jewelry	Special treasures; people of God; precious person; gifted person; truth; pride
Jewels	Certain spiritual truths; usually indicates a requirement of searching; hidden treasure
John Paul Jackson and/or other figures known for their prophetic gift	Represents prophetic gift; may represent a particular prophetic word; sometimes may be an alert to pray for him or them; may indicate your revelatory gift especially if you have been trained by him or them.
Judge	Father; act of judging or discerning
Jumping for joy	Emotional response to something very good
Jungle	Overabundance of vegetation; may indicate a tangled situation
Jury	Those who are called upon to pass judgment on others; usually made up of your peers
Kaleidoscope	May indicate that your perspective is jumbled; a new way to look at a situation; spiritual release
Kangaroo	Something that moves forward at great speed; someone who is ready to fight; carry young with them; may represent a mentor; making progress by leaps and bounds
Keep a record	To keep an account; may indicate refusal to forgive
Key(s)	Authority; access; opening things; the answer
Kid	Human child; offspring of goats; may indicate a time period in your life
King	The highest ruler; authority figure; may represent your father, boss, etc.
Kiss	Humility; intimate connection; agreement; covenant; enticement; betrayal; seduction; friend
Kitchen	Place of preparing spiritual food
Knee	Submission; worship; service; reverence; humility; stubborn; unyielding
Kneel	Prayer, humility
Knife	A spiritual weapon; smaller, less powerful than a sword; may indicate a need for additional training in the Word; used to divide, tongue, gossip; may indicate pain inflicted from a sharp tongue

Knight	One who is given authority by the King; usually portrayed as a defender; expertise in warfare; deliverer; usually travels by horse (see "Horse"); may be wordplay for night
Knit(ted)	Work done to keep separate people/things together; creativity
Knocking at death's door	In a situation that seems may end in death for someone; may indicate the death of a relationship or season of life
Koala	Seems playful but is not
Labor / delivery	Praying someone into the spirit; travail and intercession
Ladder	Ascend or descend; enable; way of escape; promotion if going up; struggle if hard
Ladybugs	Sign of overcoming; (they eat aphids that destroy plants)
Lake(s)	Church or group of people
Lamb / sheep	Innocence; purity; one who requires great care; shy person; members of a particular church; those who are followers of Jesus; humility; prosperity; responsibility; submission
Lamp	That which gives off light; gives understanding;
Lampstand	Term used for menorah; candlestick; illumination; enlightenment
Landmines	Earthly thinking or earthly mindedness; potential destruction; hidden danger
Lapis Lazuli (Gem)	Stone in the breastplate of the High Priest for the tribe of Issachar; called the stone of friendship and fidelity; aids in increasing kindness; helps with spiritual attunement
Large store	Market place; may indicate the need to take the message about Jesus to those outside of the church
Late bloomer	Someone who comes into maturity later than expected
Laughter	Refreshment, joy
Laundry room	Cleansing; getting your act together; cleaning up your life
Lava	An internal increase in pressure that bubbles up unnoticed; usually bursts forth powerfully but may be slow moving
Leaf / Leaves	Indicates life if growing; healing; covering; covenant; doctrine; self justification; prosperity or adversity; consider their condition and color; dead leaves may indicate something that has to be put away
Leaven	Kingdom spreading; sin spreading through church
Left	Has to do with your destiny; the abilities that you were given at birth; making a turn, change in spirit; rejected; may indicate westward direction;
Leg of furniture	The part of the table or chair that holds it up; support; friendship
Legs	Support; man's walk; his strength; foundation
Lemon	A machine that breaks down shortly after purchase
Leopard	Someone who never changes
Let sleeping dogs lie	Let bygones be bygones; don't bring up something that isn't relevant for the moment
Letter	Message; instruction; personal communication
Library	Research; knowledge stored up; education; Holy Bible; associated with how you use knowledge or awareness you already possess

Lice	Blood suckers; live off others; typically found in hair so may speak of a problem with the wisdom that has been displayed
License	Freedom to act; authority
Life is a dream	Life can sometimes seems as though it is not really happening; or it can seem too good to be true
Life is a roller coaster	Daily situations can be good and bad
Life is like a bowl of cherries	Can be sweet but you have to watch out for the pits
Life is like a box of chocolates	You never know what you may get!
Life seasons	God is healing past wound from that era; past jobs, homes, childhood; God repeating a lesson not learned
Light	Manifest; revealed; expose; God; Jesus
Light at the end of the tunnel	The final event turns out better than expected while going through; a way out there now appears to be hope in this situation
Light – coming thru	Hand: power of God to touch others
Light – dim	Without full knowledge or understanding
Light – flashlight	Personal knowledge or understanding; guidance
Light – off	Without understanding or manifestation
Lighthouse	Warning, prayer offered for others
Lightning	Majesty of God; God coming into activity in earth; associated with thunder, voices, earthquakes; power; instant miracle; judgment; destruction, concentrated light; power upon one area; has a great effect but does not always destroy
Lily	Popular flower during celebration of the resurrection of Jesus; immortality
Limousine	See "Car – limo"
Lion	Intimidating power; lion of Judah; devourer; great courage; aggression
Lion – attacking you	Enemy trying to bring attack; God coming against what you are doing
Lionhearted	Brave
Liver	Weighty matter; glory; heaviness; richness; goodness that flows through; purification
Living room	Formal fellowship of church or family and friends
Lizard	Someone who speaks lies from a long distance
Locked box	Solution that alludes you; something you are looking for
Locker room	Place of preparation for something; spiritual warfare
Locust	Same as grasshopper
Log cabin	Place of compassion
Look at world through rose colored glasses	Determine to look at things in the best possible way; believe the best about everyone and every situation
Looking down	Higher perspective; spiritual level
Lottery – winning	Unexpected favor coming

Love is a fragile flower	Love developing must be handled carefully so it can grow
Love is a lemon	Love can be a wonderful thing or something that causes much pain
Luxury – dept. store	God's storehouse
Lying on stomach	Signifies confidence; being able to lay it all down with no concern with what is behind you; humility; akin to falling on your face; may be a position of worship
Machine	When used as a person, indicates feeling run down, may need to refuel; something that is predictable; it important to consider the type of machine, its running condition, what it is used for
Machine guns	Powerful spiritual weapon capable of firing repeatedly
Magazine	Circular; current information; message
Maggots	Fly larvae; feed on garbage or something that has been left unattended, multiply quickly
Malachite	Believed to help in prosperity, heals the eyes, blood sugar levels, and circulatory diseases
Mall	World; reaching out to others in the marketplace; egotism or selfishness; desire for worldly goods; marketplace
Mantle	Area of spiritual gifting; protective covering
Manure	That which is of no value; nourishment for plants
Map	Directions; word of God; correction; advice
Marble	Kingdom beauty; sincerity of heart
Marble floor	Lots of polishing to get where you are; servant
Marijuana	Illegal; form of escape; may warn of taking in something negative
Mark	Distinguished; sign; identification; mark of the beast
Marriage	Covenant between a man and a woman
Marriage – on rocks	Having marital problems that may lead to divorce
Mascara	Draws attention to eyes, spiritual vision
Mask	False face
Massive	Large influence
Measurement	Often means time; if you have to go distance, it means time
Measuring stick	That which is used to measure the depth and quality of a person's character
Meat	Deep spiritual truth; source of nourishment and strength; protein
Medicine	Healing; wisdom
Melon	Head
Melting	Being reduced
Menstruation	End of cleansing, preparing for ovulation
Mental institution	Place where you are locked away in mental bondage
Mice	Thoughts; something unattended; permitted to be there; demonic; fear of something unattended; humility; not drawing attention to self
Mice and rats	Larger negative spirits; feed off garbage in your life

Microphone	Voice of God; prophetic message; authority; life purpose; influence
Microwave oven	Quick work; sudden; instant; impatient; convenience
Milk	Simple form of nourishment; simple spiritual truth; promise
Mind	Bondage
Mire	That which hinders
Mirror	God's Word; one's heart; looking at one's self; looking back; memory; past; vanity; reflection; what's going on with person in the mirror
Miscarriage	Abort; failure; loss; repentance; unjust judgment
Mist	Gentle watering; may represent the presence of God
Moaning	Complaining; travail
Mobile home	Temporary dwelling; not built to last; able to move around and take home with you
Mole	One who digs up dirt on others; hides from the light
Money	Provision; that you are going to receive favor; time
Money – black and white	Indicates greed
Money – fifty	Forgiveness of debt, cancellation of debt coming, close to time of freedom
Money – foreign	Favor in the area where that money is accepted as currency
Money – lost	Loss of favor; loss of provision
Monkey	Mocker; harasser; playful; addiction; foolishness
Monkey on back	Suffering from something that you can't seem to free yourself from; addiction
Monkey wrench	Something that causes a change
Monster	Fear that has not been dealt with; may indicate an attack of the enemy; hidden issue that you are not aware of; for children: can indicate an indefinable fear, or their ability to see in the spirit though they are not able to define what they see
Moon	Reflection of the sun (Son); femininity; cycles; controls the tides
Moonstone	Calming; good for meditation; believed to provide spiritual guidance and protection while traveling; indicates spiritual condition
Moose	Native to North America; large and strong; strong swimmers; feeds on tree branches; large ears constantly moving like radar; excellent hearing; attracts attention; big, athletic man; immovable obstacle
Mortar	Holds things together
Mosquito	Carries disease; pest; sucks blood so drains life
Motel	Temporary residence; may indicate a state of mind
Moth(s)	Eat through wool; destroy mantle
Mother	Holy Spirit; understanding; church you are associated with; actual mother; mentor; nurturer
Motorcycle	Same as bicycle but more power; unique life purpose
Mountain	The establishing of the Lord; God's presence
Mouse	Shy; timidity; underfoot; multiplies quickly; smaller version of rat (negative)
Mouth	Ability to speak for God; prophesy
Mouths to feed	Number of persons for whom you are responsible

Mud	Unpleasant things spoken; softening of solid ground; flesh; man's way; lust passion; temptation; difficulty caused by weakness of flesh
Muddy water	Confusion concerning spiritual truth
Mule	Beast of burden; hardheaded; stubborn
Museum	Blood line
Mustard tree	Place of rest, refuge
Nails	Words; wisdom; fasten; steadfast; permanent unchangeable; secure
Nakedness	Vulnerable; exposed; everything out in the open; having nothing to hide – transparent; humility
Naked – On stage	Your vulnerability is witnessed by many
Naked – try to Cover	Trying to conform to others; acting appropriately in a certain circumstance
Naked – waist down	Vulnerable in the area of fruitfulness
Naked – waist up	Vulnerable visibly, but there may not be fruit with it; one's nurturing nature being exposed
Names	Identity; consider actual name and its origin and meaning; many can be found at behindthename.com
Names in scripture	Consider the name given, the person's characteristics and accomplishments, etc.
Neck	Willingness; stiff-necked; stubborn; support; keeps you connected to the one true Light
Neck of the woods	A particular area that is very familiar
Nest	Dwelling place; self made home; birthing; rest; nurturing; safety; comfort
Net	Similar to a web, something that connects; also used to capture; what you are left with
Newspaper	Public exposure; prophecy; gossip; announcement; important events
Nightgown	Clothed for rest and intimacy; if out in the day indicates not being prepared
North	Symbol of power; majesty; spiritual judgment; heavenly; place of God's throne; above (God is above all); judgment; spiritual; symbol of power; majesty; gloomy
North wind	Undeserved favor of God; harsh, bitter cold, time of trial; judgment
Nose	Ability to know what is going on; being able to discern; busybody; nosy; meddling; strife; smell
Not in my ballpark	Not something you can afford
Numbers	See "Numbers" separate listing
Numbers doubled	Meaning of number doubled
Numbers multiplied	Meaning of number intensified
Nursing	Healing; nurturing; comfort; may be Great Spirit

Nuts	Someone who is not in their right mind; snack food that provides protein; small package that contains great benefit
Ocean	Indicates large numbers of people; may also speak of movement of Spirit
Ocean liner	Organization that is moved by the Spirit; would indicate something very large; carries large number of people; travels ocean; large church
Octopus	Many arms may indicate someone who is able to accomplish much; Jezebel spirit
Offering	That which is given freely
Office	Indicates function in Body and what you are called to do
Office building	Work, administration, performance, your function; consider the condition, location, etc.
Oil	Anointing
Old love	Old ways or temptation to go back to old ways
Old man	Old movement; wisdom
On top of head	Indicates importance; may speak of being spontaneous (off the top of my head)
One rotten apple	Spoils the whole barrel: one bad person in a group can have a negative effect on the whole group.
Onyx	Stone in the breastplate of the High Priest for the tribe of Gad; black (see "Colors") called the stone of separation, can be used for purpose of release to end a bothersome relationship.
Opal	Usually white with various iridescent colors. Can be blue, pink, green, orange (see "Colors") believed to aid in prophecy; balances chakras, used for centering self, aids teaching truths to others, called the *anchor of hope*, also called the *stone of cupid*
Orange – color	See "Colors" section for expanded definitions
Orange – fruit	Love, greatest pleasure; Son Kissed (wordplay on Sunkist); source of Vitamin C, which is very important for immune system
Out of one's mind	Not rational; not able to think in a logical manner
Outer space	Speaks of heavenlies; information about the universe
Oven	Fiery trials; testing; judgment; fire pot; heart
Owl	Night person; wisdom; considered one who announces death; clear vision; able to see in the darkness
Ox	Big, strong man; slow laborious change; hard work
Paint	Doctrine; truth or deception
Palace	Temple
Palate	Provision
Palm	Healing; giving of oneself; openness
Palm branch	Reed: in a rush; waved to show praise and adoration
Panda	Demure but deadly; religious; the black & white of a situation
Pantry	Resource; provision
Pants	Position of authority (who wears the pants); walking in what you are called to do; personal identity

Paralyzed	Unable to move; not able to function normally; circumstances choking you; may indicate not spending enough time in quiet meditation and/or contemplation; ineffectively limping along spiritually; demonic hindrance; something in your spirit is not fully functioning or operating yet
Parked car	See "Car – parked"
Parking lots	Purpose is to contain cars for a certain amount of time; there is a cost to using them
Parrot	Mockers; imitators
Parroting ideas	Simply repeating what you have heard
Party	Particular thought process; celebration; may indicate irresponsible lifestyle; consider purpose
Pastor	Leader; may represent God; may represent your literal husband
Pasture	Place of provision, rest, nourishment
Path	Beginning way of journey; trail to a particular place
Patient	Patience; one in need of healing
Paw	Unclean power
Peach	Pretty girl; joy; sweet sense of well being
Peachy	Fine; okay
Peacock	Pride; vanity; beauty
Pear	Patience; longevity; life that is enduring without calamity
Pearl	White or off-white (see "Colors"); associated with life purpose; wisdom through experience, said to quicken the law of karma; believed to bring engagements and love relationships; symbolizes the Church; Israel
Pearl(s)	God's truth; God's people; formed through suffering; aspects of truth
Pebbles	Small but makes large impact; usually smooth from continuous washing
Peg – tent	Stability; strength; denotes edge of sphere of influence; anchor; weapon (Jael of the ancient writings drove a tent peg into the head of her enemy)
Pen/pencil	Tongue; indelible words; covenant; agreement; contract; publish; record; permanent; unforgettable; gossip
Penny	Little value; sent one; good fortune
People	Note age, gifts, job, attributes of their name
People – faceless	Often represent angels, Spirit of God; other spiritual beings
People – handicapped	Those in need of assistance and/or healing
People – mentally	Aware of person though they are not seen: consider their name, relationship to you
People – nation	May speak of your need to pray for or minister to those from that Nation
People – specific	Life purpose or intercession for that group or individual
Pepper	Spicy; interesting; could indicate a person who seems to aggravate
Peridot	Stone in the breastplate of the High Priest for tribe of Simeon; gold or orange (see "Colors") believed to be a gift from the sun (Son), helps us open our spiritual sight; said to help develop inner vision and ability to look into the future; frees one of jealous thoughts; counteracts negative emotions.

Person is a rat	Someone who is a tattle tale
Person is a snake	Someone who is sneaky and mean
Off your rocker	Someone having mental problems
Out in left field	Someone not thinking in a way you feel is normal
Phoenix – bird	Egyptian mythological bird that, at death, bursts forth from its own ashes to new life; may indicate rebirth; process that destroys and then rebuilds
Phone	Prophetic gifting; speaking into the unseen realm
Physician	Healer
Piano	88 keys (see "Numbers"); musical stringed instrument that is played by keys; requires discipline; may represent harmony or lack thereof; may symbolize particular notes; agreement, resonance (as in striking a chord)
Picnic	Signifies a time of rest away from normal daily activities and includes eating outside on the ground or outdoor table; may indicate something being easy
Picture frame	Frame of mind
Picture frame – Antique	Shows that the message of what is pictured is from the past, possibly having to do with lineage; consider the time or age and condition
Picture frame – gold	Shows that you are being set up by God for something very important; or attention is drawn to show importance of what is pictured
Picture / Photo	Signifies a memory; change of perspective; inability to let go of a specific time period
Pie	Sweet; easy; impossible; just desserts; consider type (see meaning of particular "fruit")
Pier	Wordplay for peer; foundation in the spirit; place of awaiting arrival of someone or something; place of being held, tied up
Pig(s)	Unclean for food; sloppy person; uncouth personality; someone who speaks in an unclean manner; filthy; unclean; eats its own young; can be destructive; describes a person who is messy
Pill	Hard lesson to learn; someone who is especially irritating
Pillar(s)	Foundational; that which holds up something else; person of strong moral character
Pillow	Place of rest from mental anguish; intimacy (pillow talk)
Pilot	Authority; leadership; heavenly messenger
Pipe smoking	May indicate a relative; memories; deep thought; introspection; pollutant; irritant; consider how you feel about pipe smoking
Pirate	One who takes what does not belong to them; usually associated with evil, brutality
Pit	Warning of some type of trap; feeling of having no hope
Plane	Size specific, small = like car; large = like many people; movement; spiritual high places, large group or organization involved in spiritual life
Plane ticket	Grace and mercy; way is provided; obtained at a cost
Plank	Punishment (walk the plank); type of flooring (foundation); connection
Plant	The beginning of something; consider the type, condition, color;

Play by ear	To hear something musical and be able to play it
Plow	Forerun; make a way; break up hard ground; push through difficult situation; coming out of time of trial; preparation for future harvest
Plumb line	Standard; that by which all else is measured; indication of righteousness
Plunge	Leap of faith; to decide to move forward; surety; total abandon
Pocket watch	Indicates personal timing
Pogo stick	Setting free in the Lord; puts a spring in your step
Point blank	Abrupt
Poker	Game of chance; taking a risk that has a cost attached; tool used to stir up the fire; not showing true emotions (poker face)
Polar bear	Holy, pure, powerful; religious spirit; religious strength (see "Bear")
Police	Authority; protection; legalism; regulation; keeping order; may represent angelic being; God
Police car	Spiritual authority watching over your spiritual journey
Pomegranate	Symbol for fruit of the Spirit spoken of in Bible; embellishment on the skirts of the Priests
Pond	Spirit of God; anointing, or measure of anointing; community of like-minded people
Pony	Not at full strength of power and authority
Pool	Presence of Spirit of God; anointing, refreshing
Porch	Outreach and evangelism to the church; public place; revealed; exposed
Pornography	Mental preoccupation with sex; indicates inability to be intimate; continued practice brings spiritual death; fleshly desires
Porpoise	Wordplay for purpose; moves easily in the spiritual realm; fin looks like a shark; makes no noise that humans can hear; fruitful at a pace that is detrimental to health and longevity; able to nurse while pregnant
Pot	Slang (see "Marijuana"); cooking utensil; symbolic of establishing roots
Potato	Passion plant; love concealed
Potter	One who fashions another; creator
Pottery	Vessel formed by a potter; fragile until subjected to intense heat
Pottery – broken	Wounding in life; weakness in character exposed
Pour(ing)	Give of oneself; release
Power plant	Power that God has planted
Pregnancy	Inception or birth of something spiritual; soul; life purpose; new person; or through prayer; time of nurturing promise within
President	Our country's highest office; authority; wordplay for precedent, making the way for something that has not happened before, forerunning
Priest	Called Father; may signify God
Prison	Negative; bondage, restraints; result of justice being rendered
Prisoner	One who is in bondage of some kind, or who is being punished for wrongdoing
Prisoner of love	In love and unable to change how you feel

Private jet	Has to do with moving in the spiritual realm; usually privately owned; goes very high very fast
Property	Something that is owned and must be maintained
Prophet	Represents a prophetic word
Prostitute	Selling out; offering your services for money; debasing, devaluing of self
Puddles	Individual pools; selfishness; evidence of prior outpouring that has not lasted
Pumpkin	Term of endearment to a cute child; in form of jack-o-lantern: witchcraft, deception, snare, trick, witch
Purple heart	Bravery; act of courage; medal that denotes honor of self sacrifice for others
Purple light	Believed to increase power of meditation 10 times; understanding of how to pray for others
Purse / wallet	Treasure; heart; personal identity; precious; valuable, spiritually bankrupt if empty; control; life; carry all
Purple	See "Colors" section for expanded definitions
Push	Promote; to give birth to
Put yourself in someone else's shoes	Consider someone else's perspective as though it were your own
Quake	To tremble, shake; to feel the energy
Quarry	Where rock is blasted into a form that is usable; wordplay for query (to question)
Quartz Crystal	Stone in the breastplate of the High Priest for the tribe of Zebulon; believed to raise vibration, bridge the physical realm with the spiritual realm; has the ability to store and transmit energy; used for healing on all levels and for meditation
Queen	Authority; female who has power over you; may represent the feminine of God
Quilt	Comfort; usually denotes some personal aspect; covering
Rabbi	Spiritual authority to a Jewish person; teacher; mentor; Jesus
Rabbit	Sexual torment; multiplication; destructive; quietly enduring great pain; preoccupation mentally with sexual activity; spiritual suicide; soulish desires
Raccoon	Thief; disguised; one who operates in darkness
Race	Personal spiritual journey
Radio	Continuous; unrelenting; unceasing; unbelieving; tradition; hearing God
Radio tower	Broadcast; truth or error; gospel
Raft	Adrift; without any direction; aimless; no power; something you've made to keep yourself safe in storm
Railroad track	Tradition, unchanging; habit; stubborn; gospel; caution; danger
Rain	God's blessings; God's Word and the Holy Spirit outpoured; life; revival; trial
Rain – drought	Blessings withheld because of sin; without God's presence
Rainbow	God's covenant; protection
Ram	Power; authority; leadership; something that is forced
Rams	Occultic symbol for atanism; stubborn; trying to make things happen, butting in

Rapture	Revival; spiritual awakening; warning of a lack of preparation or of being left behind; depends upon your own beliefs about this event
Rat	Desensitized; deceit; filth; disease; thoughts; a diseased element in one's life; one who exposes others for their own benefit; unresolved issue that allows negative spiritual forces to feed on it
Ravens	Black in color so they can indicate darkness or enemy attack; may be a messenger; death
Razor	Thin line between two opinions; cutting instrument; cutting it too close – no room for error; living in a place of danger
Read	Gain knowledge, information; understanding; consider words seen
Read – inability	May indicate spiritual attack hindering your efforts to gain insight and understanding
Reap	Harvesting; reward of evil or righteousness
Reaper	Angels; one who gathers harvest; one who gets reward of labor
Recovery room	Place where you can recover
Recurring dream	Indicates importance of message; may show failure to have understood the message so far
Red	See "Colors" section for expanded definitions
Red – red letter day	Day of special importance and good fortune
Red – financial	Losing money
Red – paint the town	Celebrate
Red – red eye	An overnight airplane flight
Red – red herring	Distraction; takes your attention off the real issue
Red –see red	Be very angry
Red – card	Foul
Red – carpet	Royal treatment
Red – flag	Alert to danger
Red – lips	Huge wisdom, wisdom beyond your ability
Reed	Frailty; instability; weak spiritually; affliction
Refine	Purifying trials
Refrigerator	Where you store up your spiritual food; heart; motive; attitude; thoughts
Refrigerator – spoiled food	Harboring a grudge; negative thoughts and desires
Reins	Symbols of heart motives; pull to a halt; stop what you're doing; ability to control direction
Remote control	Power over a situation or the desire to have control when you are not directly involved
Rend	Grief; anger; schism; division
Repeated action	God is repeating what you have not listened to; establishing whatever issue is addressed in the dream
Repeated dream	Confirms that the dream is from God and the message given will come to pass

Restaurant	Atmosphere is important; where spiritual food is served to many; reaching out to lost; place of service; where you eat; there is a cost to what you get
Rhinoceros	Personality that is rough; someone who is critical; has a large horn that may lead you to think he or she has authority; nosy person who pushes his or her way in; bossy
Ribs	Indicate someone close to the heart; may represent woman; or the church
Rick Joyner	Prophetic; apostolic; corporate leadership; teacher; may be an alert to pray for him; may indicate your revelatory gift especially if you have been trained by him.
Right	Showing you to do the right thing; encouraging you to go the correct way; concerns the amount of faith you have; authority; power; the strength of man or flesh; power of God accepted; that which is natural (a change in the natural = a right turn)
Right side of brain	The side that controls creativity
Right wing	Speaks of one's political beliefs
Ring	Symbol of covenant; authority; a ring with gems can indicate precious promises; consider type of gem and its color, condition, value, etc.
Ring finger	Pastor
Ring – off finger	Broken covenant, relationship, freedom
Ring – on finger	Indicates being in a covenant, relationship; may indicate authority in a situation
River	Life giving flow; Spirit of God; move of God
River – dry riverbed	Legalism; religious behavior
Riverboat	Usually powered by steam or wheel on water; indicates something moving in the spirit; carries a lot of people though usually moves slowly
Road	Spiritual path; established direction; consider condition of road and direction
Robber	Poverty; one who takes what does not belong to him; draining energy
Robbery	Violation; been cheated
Robe	Covering; note the color
Rock	Jesus; wise foundation
Rocket	Goes up very fast; if not careful could burn up
Rocket ship	Represents power, pioneering, great spiritual heights, something so far away it may it may seem strange at first
Rocking chair	Past memories; meditation; rest; retirement; prayer
Rod	Rule; chastening; guidance; crushing; seal of priesthood protection; discipline; correction
Roll	Ease of journey
Roller coaster	Worldly ride; life's ups and downs; inability to walk firmly grounded
Roller skates	Gliding; speed; fast; swift advancement; skillful
Rolling in dough	Having a lot of money
Rolling stone	Active; one who does not remain in one place for long

Roof	May speak of your spiritual leaders or the belief system you are under; covering; protection; mind; thought; heavenly revelation
Room	A particular area of your own heart
Room – no walls	Ability to see in the sprit realm; abundant provision; no limits; no boundaries; experiencing a vision
Room – secret	Strongholds; additional provision that you are not aware of; area of your own heart that you have not opened up before
Rooster	Cocky; rising; morning; wake-up call; may indicate a wake-up call; arrogant person; may indicate someone who is angry; something that is not true
Root	Offspring source; attitude; motives
Rope	Three strand cord – not easily broken
Rose	Denotes healing; romance; love; consider color, condition and source
Rose Quartz	Pink (see "Colors"); said to bring more love, rejuvenate skin
Rowboat/row	Life purpose doing the work of man; earnest prayer; spiritual labor
Ruby	Red (see "Colors"); spiritual wisdom; aids in focusing; confidence, called the *stone of life and energy*; valuable deep red gem; spiritual wisdom
Rug	Covering; deception or cover up
Runner / Running	Swiftness; movement; striving; working out one's salvation; running away is avoidance
Rut	Stuck in tradition; stuck in a rut
Sailboat	Life purpose totally dependent on the wind of the Spirit; leaders blown about by every wind of doctrine; unstable; those driven by waves of humanity rather than God
Salt	Incorruptibility; preserve; seasoning; acceptable; godliness; divine nature; induces thirst
Sand	Flesh; improper foundation; weakness; hindrance; large numbers of people; passage of time; irritant
Sandals	Spiritual journey; aid but do not hide your walk
Sandstone	Breaks easily; looks strong from a distance but doesn't last long; will crumble
Sapphire	Dark blue (see "Colors"); sometimes used to treat mental illness, said to attract good people, calm the nerves, help in meditation; give pure insight and spiritual truth; called the *stone of chastity*; may represent the soul
Satellite	Receiving revelation
Scales	Justice; judgment; balance
Scarecrow	Protector of crops; one who seeks spiritual wisdom
Scarf	Covering; mantle; gift
Scepter	Authority; permission
School	Church; place of teaching and discipleship; training
School – College	Highest level of learning; promotion in the Spirit; strong meat
School – Elementary	Beginning level of walk with God; milk
School – Middle or Jr. High	Level of maturity of person or teaching being given or received, or of one's own walk

School High school	Promotion in level of dreamer to a higher level; or teaching being given or received
School is a gateway to adulthood	Education gives an opportunity for maturity
School yard	Freedom from training is coming
Scissors	Cutting tool; may indicate the need to cut something out of your life; usually controlled; cutting remarks
Scorpion	Stinging; poisonous; small but packs a punch; may indicate witchcraft coming against you
Scraggly	Gift not well kept
Scribe	Teachers with understanding or application; recording of what is happening
Scroll	Torah; ancient wisdom; message; Word of God; religious teachings
Sea	Humanity; people; nations
Sea horse	Prophetic power
Sea of sadness	Surrounded by sadness that seems to have no end
Seal	Sealing up; ceiling; navy seal symbolizes increased training; nose of seal means to go under for a long time, occult; takes a long time to remove; may indicate the identity of one who produced seal
Seasons	Season you are coming out of; notice location, time, buildings, etc
Seat	Position
Seed	Word of God, faith, kingdom
Seize the day.	Take the opportunities each day.
Serpent	Satan; also see "Snake"
Sex with old lover	Warning that you may be desiring to go back to the way it was with a previous person
Sex with spouse	Intimacy, communication
Sexual encounter	May be a cleansing dream; reveals soulish desires; may indicate something that is to come; desire for intimacy
Shack	Poor; on vacation; may indicate an uncommitted relationship
Shade	Relief from heat of day; protection; covering
Shadows	Something hidden; may indicate darkness; warning of impending danger; evidence of a person or thing that blocks the light
Shark(s)	People who are dangerous; usually operate below the surface; hustler who strikes a devastating blow if allowed to get close
Sheaves	Harvest
Sheep	People (see "Lamb / sheep")
Sheepish	Embarrassed
Shekinah	Glory of God; Presence of God
Shepherd	God; one who feeds, guards, protects, guides; one who has authority over the sheep
Shield	Weapon of warfare; protection; guard against accusation
Ship	Something that has a large impact; able to affect large numbers of people; leadership

74

Shipwreck	Organization that has been rendered ineffective or suffered destruction
Shoe	Being prepared to walk in your calling; to share the gospel of peace; different types of shoes can indicate different types of life passions or destinies
Shoe – no shoes	No peace; connected with creation; informal; relaxed
Shoe – does not fit	Means you are trying to walk in something you're not called to, or are not equipped to operate in
Shoots	Evidence of new growth beginning; small but packed with nutrition
Shopping center	Variety, either spiritual or soulish
Shopping mall	A movement, a group of ministries
Shore	Calling to missions
Shorts	If inappropriate for situation shows you are not prepared; cut-offs indicate something you have altered for your own convenience; being comfortable; can indicate a destiny cut short or only partially fulfilled
Shoulder	Ability to bear weight for someone else; strength; government, authority
Shower – clogged	Communication with God is stopped up
Showering	Time of total cleansing; getting completely honest with God and receiving cleansing; remove cares of the world
Shrew	Nagger, complainer (especially used to refer to a woman)
Shrimp	Small person
Sick as a dog	Terribly ill
Side	Area of vulnerability; place of friendship; new relationship
Signature	Identifying mark; indicates identity; proof of agreement
Signet	Symbol that signifies identity and authority; used to make a seal
Silence screams	To be so aware of the lack of sound
Singing song	Evidence of peace; worship; building oneself up; note words if a new song
Sink	To go down; place of cleansing
Sitting	Time of rest; position of authority; take note of type and color of chair and where it is
Sitting – Indian style	Contemplative meditation; communing with God; may indicate a religious spirit or pseudo spirituality
Sitting – on toilet	Going through a time of cleansing; ridding self of toxins; spiritual purification
Skateboard	Agility; draws the young
Skirts	Rejoicing; covering; consider color and condition
Skunk	Disliked person; fear of man; stinky situation; religious spirit
Sky scraper	Potential for high responsibility; prophetic church with great power; high spiritual destiny
Sleigh	Power in ability to live a holy life (horse drawn); ability to move in great favor
Sloth	Lazy person
Small	Humble
Small toe	Out of balance in a small way

Smoke	Presence of God; intercession; evidence of fire
Snail	Physically very slow person
Snake	Has to do with false words or beliefs; lies that have been told; wordplay for long tail, long tale; deception; wisdom; healing; Caduceus (doctor's symbol) rebelliousness; cleverness; temptation
Snake / serpent	Cunning person
Snake bite	A lack of awareness; caught off guard
Snake – nonpoisonous	Cleverness; proceeding with discernment
Snake – poisonous	Pertains to swift retaliation or attacks
Snake – python	Squeezes the life out of you; spirit that causes lethargy; can represent ancestral communication with the dead
Snake – white	Spirit of religion
Snapping turtle	Presence of God
Snow	Reveals God's favor on you; refreshing; righteousness; purity; favor
Soaring / flying	High spiritual activity, going to new heights
Soldier	One who is prepared for battle; angelic being; one who fights at the direction of another; member of military forces; note what type of uniform
Someone is a 10	You feel a person is perfect in every way
Something comes back to bite you	Consequences of your actions that are unpleasant
Hard to swallow	When something is hard to believe or hard to accept
Sour grapes	Envy
South	Symbol of quietness of earth; opposite of north wind; beneath; down; natural
South wind	Blows from God to release fragrance of spices; refreshing; freedom from spiritual bondage
Spaceship	Going to the highest levels with God
Sparrow	Simplicity
Spear	Weapon that allows for fighting with some distance between you and enemy; getting the point
Speed boat	Moves fast and doesn't last long; can be very exciting; dangerous; doesn't cover anybody for long; careless with anointing
Speedo	Clothing for moving in the water; may indicate vulnerability or agility and speed in moving in the spirit
Spices	Consider type; color; condition; fragrance; medicinal value, and / or cost
Spices – aloes*	Intimacy; healing of burns; healing of skin
Spices – calamus*	Uprightness
Spices – cassia*	Homage to God alone
Spices – cinnamon*	Holiness of heart
Spices – frankincense	Purity; spiritual understanding

Spices – galbanum*	Worship, praise, adoration and thanksgiving
Spices – henna	Forgiveness
Spices – myrrh	Understanding and compassion; obedience unto death; courage; energy
Spices – onycha*	Authority
Spices – saffron*	Faith
Spices – spikenard*	Light
Spices – stacte*	Truth with mercy
Spices – vanilla	Peace (natural – sweet, calming effect upon the body)
Spider	Small but powerful; often poisonous; may indicate an attack of dark forces; one who lures; one who spins a web of deceit
Spider web	Something put in place by the enemy to catch you or impede your progress; sticky situation that could lead to your harm
Spleen	Has to do with the immune system; compassion; laughter; self control
Spoon-feed	Make lessons very easy; not make students work for themselves
Sports field	Place to learn to conquer or how to play as part of a team
Spring	Time of new beginning; new life; a shift in season
Springs	Vehicle of forward progress; sets free (or lets go free)
Squeaky wheel gets the grease.	Noisy people get attention; those who keep bringing an issue to the forefront are more likely to get something done about it
Squirrel	Your ability to prepare for the future; hides away things for later; strange behavior
Stadium	Holds large numbers of people; indicates having a great impact; influence masses
Stagecoach	Transportation of olden days; very hard way to travel
Stairs	Means of getting to higher or lower levels; may want to consider number of stairs or number of floors
Stairs – down	Losing ground; going backward
Stairs – Narrow	Narrow is the way; your progress requires strict adherence to certain boundaries or rules
Stairs – No railing	Must be traveled carefully; progress entails a certain amount of danger
Stairs – railing	Boundaries; something to hold on to as you progress
Stairs – up	An opening; making progress in the Spirit; advancing
Stairs – with light	God's direction in your life, even though it is hard to understand
Stairway	Indicates progression on your spiritual journey; similar to a portal in that it is a way to go higher but it requires you to work at it; consider whether going up or down
Stamp	Price paid to get a message out
Starfish	Grace for regeneration
Stars	Associated with your fortune (whether good or bad); someone who has made great accomplishment; may indicate a sign from heaven

Steel	Strong; unwavering; strengthened by fire of trial
Steel building	Without sides: potential has not been realized yet
Steering wheel	Element of control; instrument of control
Stethoscope	Ability to hear from the heart level; spiritual sensitivity
Sticking out hand	Desire for relationship
Stillborn child	Something that was prepared for, or anticipated, has died
Sting	Painful words; hurt that causes a deep burning; something rings true
Stitch in time saves nine	Taking early action or precautions keeps you from having serious problems later
Stomach	Humility; organ of digestion; that which is taken in as nourishment is processed
Stomp foot	Taking authority over enemy
Stone	Symbol of foundation; may refer to a jewel; may indicate being judgmental
Stop and smell the roses	Indicates your need to take time to enjoy simple pleasure in life
Store	Where you go to buy things you need; there is a cost for what is obtained there
Stork	Unclean food; generational issue
Storms	Time of turmoil or testing; period of unrest
Storms – black	Usually indicate they are from enemy
Storms – white	Means that what is happening is allowed by God for His purpose
Stranger	That which is unknown to you
Straw	That which is of little value; brittle; that which is used to drink; wordplay of "suck up"
Strawberry	Goodness; divine virtue and healing; cleansing; humility, goodness, excellence
Stream(s)	Particular life purpose group; way of thinking about spiritual things
Street	Path; usually paved and indicates a particular way to travel
Streetcar	See "Car – streetcar"
Stronghold	Something that you believe to be true even though it is not really true
Stubble	That which is left over when harvest is complete; of no value
Stubs	Small part of what originally existed
Stumble	To fall to temptation; to get out of step; to believe a lie
Stumbling block	Something or someone whom you allow to affect your decision making
Stump	Evidence of some former living thing being cut down
Submarine	Weapon that operates beneath the surface; hidden but powerful
Subway	Tunnel transportation; usually moving quickly; must pay a price to travel; may indicate progress that is being made that is not readily apparent
Suck the marrow	Enjoy life to the fullest
Suitcases	Indicate packing belongings for a trip; putting your stuff in one place

Surface	Becoming visible
Surfing	Moving quickly through things without a lot of commitment; looking briefly
Surgery	The need for something to be removed; the act of cutting something off; may indicate the need for some type of repair to be done within yourself
Swallow(ing)	Something that you have decided to believe; taking in nourishment; falling for a trick
Sweat	Man's effort; may indicate a time of struggle; getting rid of toxins would indicate going through a time of cleansing; consider cause of the sweat: exertion, fever, shame, embarrassment
Swelling	Indicates some type of attack; may also speak of ego, pride; consider part affected
Swimming	Spiritual activity; serving God; operating in the gifts of the Spirit; notice color of water
Swimming pool	Church; home; spiritual place; God's blessing; dwelling of the Spirit
Swim wear	Preparation for moving in the spirit
Sword	Word of God; weapon of close hand to hand warfare; sharp and powerful
Table	Place of fellowship; where spiritual nourishment is taken in
Tablet	See scroll
Tail	False prophet; that which is in past; the end of something; cowardice; wordplay for tale, or lie
Tarantula	Positive meaning can be wild celebratory spirit; negative same as spider
Tares	Sons of the wicked one; weeds; the proud
Target	What you are aiming for
Tattoo	Identification; mark put on skin purposely to convey a particular meaning; consider the tattoo itself to determine the meaning; mark position on body, color, picture or words; can signify belonging
Taxi	See "Car – taxi"
Tea	Drink that can be relaxing; usually consumed during fellowship
Tearing	Act of repentance
Tears	Indication of sadness or joy; washing of eyes that shows cleansing of spiritual vision
Teddy bear	Comfort; gift; used to describe a male who is generally physically large but has a sweet spirit and big heart
Teeth	One's ability to understand or come to a conclusion; chew on something and make a decision; wisdom
Teeth – eye teeth	Wisdom that has to do with spiritual vision
Teeth – hair on	Maturity
Teeth – Incisor	Ability to make decisions, decisiveness with understanding
Teeth – Wisdom	Wisdom; may be painful; ability to act in wisdom
Telescope	To see afar off; spiritual insight; being able to see into the future
Television	Wordplay for "tell a vision;" receiving information by being tuned in; may indicate worldly entertainment
Temple	The dwelling place of spiritual energy; your physical body
Tent	Temporary but can lead to what is permanent

Termites	That which gnaws away and destroys if not dealt with; generally speaks of a hidden irritation that does more damage than is easily detected
Test	Undergoing a time of testing
Test – not prepared	Feeling you are not ready to undergo whatever task you have been given
Test – passed	You have learned the lesson you were given; you have responded correctly to a situation
Thanks from the bottom of your heart	Feeling intense thankfulness and expressing it passionately or enthusiastically
The Big Apple	New York City
Theater	God is about to show you something; vision
Thigh	Area of strongest bone in the body; authority; identity; faith; covenant
Thirst	Desire for water; indicates a body's need for hydration
Thorns and thistles	Cares, concerns, and riches of the world
Three measures	Body, soul, spirit
Three strikes and you're out	To repeatedly fail and have no other chances given
Threshing floor	Place of wrestling with God; where you go to get clarity of beliefs
Throat	Swallowing takes place; voice box is located; airway; has to do with speech
Throne	Position of authority; usually reserved for a monarch; sometimes used to refer to a toilet
Thrown for a loop	Something that has been hard for you to accept or mentally process
Thumb	Apostolic authority (apostolic gifting); authority to influence; touches all of the other fingers or gifts in service and administration; holds together a fist – strength
Thunder	Spiritual warning of issues that are awaiting; loudness of a voice; God's voice
Ticker problems	Heart problem
Tiger	Aggressive person (good meaning); may indicate someone using the power of the soul; someone who is stubborn; controlling spirit
Time	Money
Time is money	Time is a precious and valuable thing
Tires	Carries your life and or job/life purpose somewhere
Tires flat	Holy Spirit not in it
Titanic	Pride; seemingly unsinkable; a plan that is not going to work out well
To see red	To be angry
Toad	dark spirit; enchantment; magic; prince that has not been revealed
Toe	See "Big toe" and "Small toe"
Toilet paper	Provision for cleaning up a mess
Tomato	Kindness; heart of God; big heartedness; generosity, undefiled conscience; compassion and mercy

Tongue	Speech; language used; heavenly language; something that should not be said
Tooth	May indicate your words; (see "Teeth")
Top dog	Best person; person or group in position of highest authority
Topaz	Sky blue (see "Colors")
Torch	Illumination in darkness; God; deep felt feelings for someone; light that comes from fire
Tornadoes – dark	From enemy; destruction; dark; invokes fear
Tornadoes – white	Indicates it has been allowed by God for your benefit; may indicate prayers being pulled up to heaven
Tower	Place of a watchman; higher perspective; place of safety; change coming in situation
Tractor	Laborious effort; power to do; plow; power to plow
Trailer park	Mobile home; group or organization that is transient; rest and relax
Train	May indicate a move of God; carrying large amount of supplies; training or education; large group or large church; mostly goes in one direction; divided in cars = groups or people in that movement
Train – getting on	Need training; getting training
Treasure	Indication of what means most to you; location of your heart
Treasure chest	God is taking you to new levels of treasures in Him
Tree(s)	Those in leadership; mature faith; one who has deep roots and is stable; providing for others
Tree – different types	Consider characteristics, location, condition; e.g., willow = sorrow
Tree house	Hidden, simple place in God
Triple number	When a number is tripled (444; 666; etc) it gives added dimension and scope; consider the meaning of the individual number (see "Numbers" section)
Truck	Consider type, color, and condition
Truck – 18 wheeler	Blessing, provision
Truck – pickup	Evangelist; word play for "pick up" as in "pick up" people: a destiny you have to help others, whether through encouragement or meeting their needs through physical transportation or other help
Trumpet	Heavenly message; warning; announcement; ego or egotistical behavior
Tugboat	Organization that is known to help others
Tumbleweed	Being blown about without clear direction for life
Tunnel	A way through that may seem dark and scary; no turning back; passage; transition; way of escape; trial; hope
Turkey	Wisdom; thanksgiving; provision; foolishness; not too smart
Turquoise	Called the stone of friendship; symbol of spiritual nature; (see "Colors")

Turtle	Physically slow person; hard shell; hides; closed in; comfort; peace; protection; snappy; dwells in deep; longevity; introverted personality; mother heart of God
Two heads are better than one	Better to have someone else's perspective than just your own
Two-story house	Place with a higher level of anointing
UFO	Heavenly messenger; alien; something that you can't identify
Umbrella	Preparation for trial; covering; protection when things begin to fall
Underdog	The weaker party in a competition
Underwater	Deep things in the spirit
Underwear	Degree of vulnerability, but you wont be very reproductive that way
Unicorn	Purity; virginity; mysterious; magical; ancient mysteries; Jesus
United States	Governmental; consider location
Upside-down	Sometimes said of Kingdom life, i.e., give to receive, lose to win, love when hated; unusual; a totally different perspective; unexpected direction; something you are not called to; a group or organization that seems worldly that you had expected to be spiritual
Upstairs	Going higher in the Spirit; of the Spirit; Upper room; Pentecost; thought
Urchin	Trouble-maker; mischievous; (esp. used of or about children)
Vaccination	Protection from invading forces; depends upon your feelings toward vaccinations
Vacuum	Cleaning up; may indicate the need to for spiritual house cleaning; warning not to get sucked into something
Vampire	A person that sucks the life out of another; may warn against a relationship or a coming attack by dark forces
Van	Group endeavor; consider color and condition
Vanilla	See "Spices"
Vegetable	A quadriplegic; nutritious food
Vegetable crisper	Refreshing
Veil	Caution to look beyond what is seen; hides something; usually covers face, may indicate you are not seeing the truth about someone in their behavior
Venom	Poison that is released during wounding; sharp painful words that do lasting damage; emotions that are not correct; what develops from unresolved negative emotions
Video	Vision
Vine	Nation of Israel; Church; source or people
Vinegar	Something that is hard to take; sour personality
Violin	Compassion; sympathy
Vision	Ability to see
Vision – behind	Historic vision; earlier call in life
Vomit(ing)	Something taken in but not digested, something bad for you being expelled; may indicate deliverance
Vultures	Evidence of something dying or dead; feed off dead bodies
Walking	Your spiritual walk; individual lifestyle

Walking out of Limo	Walking out of dark night of soul
Walking out of marsh	Going from a time of struggle to better times
Wall	Boundary; may be protection; hindrance; obstacle; confinement
Wallet	Personal identity; usually contains your money, favor
War	Argument; problem between people, etc., that not been settled
Warehouse	Place of provision and storage
Warfare	Engagement in battle; fighting while sleeping may accomplish what is fought over
Warning	Spoken warning
Warrior	Prayer warrior; one who fights for another or for a cause; protector
Washing	Reading the Word of God; going through purification process; cleaning up one's act; consider what is being washed (body, clothes, car, etc.);
Washing hands	Relationship with God being put into right perspective; refusing to take responsibility
Watch(ing)	Seeing what is coming; being given a new perspective
Watching self	Warning, not being spirit led; God is making double emphasis; you are being shown something about yourself that you would be unable to see otherwise
Watchman	One who watches in the spirit for indication of movement, whether of God or the enemy, with the intent of warning others of danger; sounds the alarm; intercessor
Water	Holy Spirit; a problem; when moving, indicates God at work; when still, may represent spiritual community; if stagnant, may indicate spiritual life which has grown dull from neglect
Water – deep	Deeper in Spirit
Water – frozen	Religious spirit operating to hinder move of Holy Spirit
Water – muddy	Confusion
Water – ocean	See "Ocean"
Water – ponds	See "Pond"
Water – river	See "River"
Water – sea	Humanity
Water – swimming pool	Particular place where God is moving; personal anointing
Water under the bridge	Situations that have happened that cannot be changed
Water – waves	Waves of humanity; rhythmic patterns; may speak of timing
Wax	Something or someone that is pliable; able to be molded
Weasel	Avoider
Weasel out of something	Use cunning to avoid some responsibility
Weatherman	Predicts future
Weaving	Done by hand
Wedding dress	Covenant; deep relationship

Weeds	Negative thoughts that choke out spiritual life; obstacles or issues that need to be removed
Weeping	Indicates deep sorrow; travail; intercession
Well	Deep reserves; spiritual source
West	Symbol of evening; going down of the sun; sunset; day closing; day's end; revival; the cross
West wind	Wisdom
Whale	Deep spiritual things; spiritual generosity; big spiritual impact; big spiritual issue; group is called a pod; under the surface; play on words for "Wales" (such as in revival); enormous; derogatory term used to denote a very fat person; exaggeration
Wheat field	Harvest
Wheelchair	Healing; limited mobility; symbolic of loss of ability to maneuver under own will; depending on injury, may signify a temporary or permanent condition
Wheels	Coming full circle; closure; ease of movement
Whirlwind	Confusion; great movement that causes one to be disoriented
Whisper	Hearing; intimate
White	See "Colors" section for expanded definitions
White as snow	Pure
White elephant	Possession that costs more than it is worth
White flag	Truce
White glove inspection	To be put to the test down to the last detail
White heat	State of intense enthusiasm, anger, devotion, or passion
White knight	Rescuer
White lightning	Home-made alcoholic beverages
White monsters	There is a way that seems right
Whiteout	Covers up mistakes; snowing so hard you can't see anything but the snow
White robes	Heavenly garments
White sale	Sale of linens, bed and bath items
White wash	To try to cover up defects; make something sound better than it is
White water	The rough flowing waters of rapids and waterfalls
Whited sepulcher	Those who appear good on the outside but are evil inside
Wick	Burning; that which allows illumination to come
Widow	One is alone due to death of relationship
Wife	Literal wife, Holy Spirit; local fellowship
Wind	When destroying things, it is a warning; can indicate the wind of God
Wind chimes	Harmony that comes from moving in the Spirit
Wind – dark	May indicate an attack from the enemy
Wind – white	May indicate it is from God
Window	Vision; ability to see in the Spirit; season of opportunity; revelation; openness; blessings from heaven; revealed truth; prophecy

Wine	Blood of Jesus; spiritual satisfaction; relaxation or need of it
Wine press	Place where doctrine is produced; could be false; pressed out separation
Wine skins	Local church; your belief system
Wing(s)	That which lifts you up in flight; also that which offers protection (under His wings)
Winnowing	Allowing the spirit to sift out ideas, thoughts, etc., that you need to get rid of
Winter	Barren; death; dormant; waiting; cold and unfriendly
Wisdom teeth	Generally denotes age and the wisdom acquired with it; acting with wisdom or losing wisdom
Witch	Rebellion; slander; worldly church; may be positive in the use of gifts for helping; negative if used for purposes of harm; magic
Wolf(ves)	False teachers; devourers; someone looking for personal gain; witchcraft; aggressive person (bad meaning); false authorities; pick on the weak
Woman / women	Holy Spirit; actual person; the church; feminine side of God; literal sisters or female relatives; female members of your fellowship; angelic beings
Womb	Place where new thing (idea, life purpose, gift, etc.) is nurtured and allowed to develop until the time that it is to be birthed
Wood	Idolatry; human effort; fleshly; occultic carved images; false fronts
Wood	Wordplay for would
Wooden tables	Compassion sets the way for many; platforms for life purpose
Woodpecker	Critical spirit that finds fault in leaders
Work like a dog	Work really hard
Work shed	Place of development; being worked on
Worm	Critical to fruitful harvest as they perfect the soil; devourer, pest; lowest, most hated person; filthiness of flesh; sin; evil
Worm – in earth	Humility
Wounds	Injury; consider location for deeper meaning
Wreath	Honor, accomplishment; celebration; consider type, season, elements, location
Wreck	Warning of natural or spiritual distress and attack
Wrestling	Striving; deliverance; resistance; controlling spirit
X-ray	Ability to see inside someone else to see who they really are; intuition; insightful
Yacht	Affluent group, organization, or church
Yard	Your life; your sphere of influence
Yard – back	In the past; behind you; memory
Yard – front	Future; prophecy or future events; in the presence of
Year	A period of blessing or judgment; revolution of time
Yeast	Leavening; something that infiltrates; may indicate increase; sin
Yellow	Symbol of quarantine; marks danger; see "Colors" section for expanded definitions
Yellow light	Proceed with caution
Yellow streak	Someone who is afraid

Yellow to holistic healers	Peace
Yellow-bellied lizard	Coward
Yoke	Servitude; slavery; total union; binding together
You had better pull your socks up	Encouragement to keep going forward
You have deep roots in an area	You have established relationships in a particular area
You have had your heart stolen	You have fallen in love
You're at a crossroads in life	A time when you need to make important decisions that have a great impact on your life
Young girl	Someone young in her faith; may indicate a new life purpose
Zebra	Same as horse but have religious spirit or soul issues; someone imprisoned
Zion	God's ruler ship; kingship; Israel
Zipper	Open or seal something
Zircon	Stone in the breastplate of the High Priest for the tribe of Joseph; gives the ability to read images and symbols, considered a stone for communication with angels; believed to give safe passage to travelers
Zoo	Confusion; chaos; noisy

* Spices meanings adapted from the following book:
Anna Rountree. The Heavens Opened. Lake Mary, FL: Creation House, 1999

Colors

"and God said, This is the token of the covenant which I make between Me and you and every living creature that is with you, for all future generations: I set my rainbow [of colors] in the cloud, and it shall be for a sign of a covenant between Me and the earth."

Genesis 9: 12-13

Colors

It is important to be aware that the symbolism of colors varies with different cultures and ethnic groups. Those offered below are the most commonly used in American dream interpretation.

Colors	Positive	Negative
Amber	Believed to ground and stabilize; acts as a filter; radiates light and heat; holiness	Contamination; idolatry
Black	Creation; creativity; rebirth; new possibilities; new life; earth; authority; power; health (hair) sophistication; elegance; formal	Death, despair, defeat; mind, will, or emotion ruling over spirit; evil; judgment; famine; sin; ignorance; tainted; impure; wicked; secrecy;
Blue	Eternity, healing, hope, sky, uplifting feelings Revelation; Holy Spirit; heavenly visitation; communion; youth; spirituality; truth; peace; tranquility; loyalty; productivity; justice; perseverance; vigilance	Depression; singing the blues; anxiety, isolation being cold emotionally; being cold due to temperature
Brass	Word of God; strength; soul	Soul; temporal; hardness of heart; judgment of sin; words of men
Bronze	Soft metal; soul; temporal	
Brown	Acceptance; warmth; success; earth; foundations; compassion; order; convention; solid; reliable; nature; humility	Disgust, disappointment; humanism; sad; wistful; compromise; false compassion
Brown (Light)	Genuineness	
Copper	Soul; temporal	
Cyan	Will; fasting	
Gold/amber	Holiness; purity; precious; high value; meant to adorn, not to hold things; purity of what God is doing; wealth; prosperity; wisdom; deity; spiritual truth; God's presence	Licentiousness; sensuality; idolatry; legalism
Gray	Comfort; mystery; hope obscured; hiddenness; security; maturity; old age; beauty of old age; repentance; purification	Weakness; sadness and confusion; ash; of little worth; mourning; mixture of black and white (consider both meanings); deception

Colors	Positive	Negative
Green	Life, new beginnings, nature; fertility; well being; improved vision; calming; refreshing; wealth; new at something; conscience	Jealous; envy; pride; bad luck; immature
Indigo	Spiritual fulfillment; philosophy or deep science; calm; intuition; meditation; deep contemplation	
Ivory	Throne; house; bed; body parts (i.e., neck, belly)	Somewhat clouded from truth; detachment; aloofness
Magenta	Emotion; giving	
Orange	Humility; beauty; vitality; endurance; perseverance	Brashness; stubbornness; rebellion; witchcraft
Pastels	Childlikeness	Can represent immaturity or pretending
Pink	Health; joy; in the pink; optimism; love; femininity; passion; beauty; tranquility	Illness; weakness; immaturity
Platinum	Rarer; less used; purity of what man is doing	
Purple	Royalty; reigning in power; bravery; authority; mystical or sacred vision; spiritual development; honor or privilege of highest order; luxury; intercession	Domination; manipulation; dictator; humanism illegitimate or false authority; artificial; loss of appetite
Red	Love; blood of forgiveness; wisdom; anointing; praying; redemption; grace; action; confidence; courage; emotional intensity; valor; hardiness	Anger; war
Silver	Redemption; grace; mercy	Legalism; soul
Violet	Associated with great spirituality or dedication; at one with God (may be used for white)	
White	Purity, innocence, sterility; neutral; light	Religious spirit; false piety
Yellow/gold	Wisdom, nature of God; renewed mind; courage; hope; gifting; joy happiness; intellectual energy; optimism; concentration; speedy metabolism	Cowardice fear; intellectual control; intellectual pride

Numbers

"So teach us to number our days that we may get us a heart of wisdom."

Psalms 90:12

Numbers

Numbers are a language in themselves. Having never been a "numbers person", interpreting the meaning of numbers used in dreams or throughout the day has always been a chore for me, but when God speaks, He always makes His message known. The following chart(s) and information are offered to give you some ideas of how numbers are used in the ancient writings along with their understood meanings. You will also find information on their connection with the meanings of the letters of the Hebrew alephbet.

It is common practice to take a two or more digit number and add the digits together to determine the definition of the final sum. This addition is continued until you arrive at a single digit number between 1 and 9.

I am of the opinion that you should first consider the number in the form it is given, using the numbers individually as spoken. For example: the number 343 would be spoken three hundred and forty three (300, 40, and 3). My first practice would be to consider the meaning of the number 300, then the meaning of the number 40, and finally the meaning of the number 3. In my experience, the answer will be found when considering the phrase or context of the three definitions.

Secondly, I would also consider the definition of the number 10 which is the sum of the three numbers (3+4+3), noting that the true sum would be 1 if following the practice of adding until you get a one digit number (1+0=1). It is my opinion that this practice often leaves out the meat of the meaning, narrowing it down too far.

It has been said that you should look at Bible verses that coincide with the numbers, but I would advise to first ask if that is what the numbers refer to, and if so, ask that the book be revealed to you. This protects you from picking the Scriptural reference you like best, rather than receiving a clearly spoken message.

NUMBER	Positive Meanings	Negative Meanings
1	God; unity; new beginnings; harmony	
2	Union; witnessing; multiplication	Division; judgment; split
3	Divine completeness and perfection; Godhead; triune God; conform	
4	Creation; the world; God's creative works; rule or reign; universality; four (4) winds; four (4) corners of the earth; four (4) living creatures	
5	Grace; god's goodness; Pentateuch; serve; work; grace; redemption	

NUMBER	Positive Meanings	Negative Meanings
6	Man	Weakness of man; manifestation of sin; evils of Satan; image; man
7	Resurrection; spiritual completeness; from the Father; complete; perfection	
8	New birth; new beginnings; teacher; put off (circumcision)	
9	Fruit of the Spirit; divine completeness from the Father; evangelist; fruit; harvest; new birth into Kingdom; like midwife (evangelist)	Apocalypse; Satan; judgment; Antichrist
10	Testimony; law and responsibility; journey; pastor; wilderness; weigh or measure for the specific purpose of rejecting or accepting	
11	Revelation; transition; prophet; witness; elect; enlightenment; standing in the gap	Disorder and judgment; transition
12	Governmental perfection; apostle; government	
13	Love; one (echad); age of bar mitzvah	Apostasy; depravity and rebellion
14	Deliverance; salvation; double anointing	
15	Rest; mercy; pardon; reprieve	
16	Love; established beginnings	
17	Victory; election; the elect	
18	Established blessing; established judgment; life	Bondage
19	Faith	
10K - 19K	Measures things to determine size, whether large or small	
20	Holy (depending on context); redemption	Divide or judge something; unholy (depending on context)
20K	something very holy; or a big decision to be made	
21		Exceeding sinfulness of sin
22	Light	
23		Death
24	The priesthood; elders around the throne;	
25	Begin life purpose training; repentance; the forgiving of sins	
26	God; gospel of Christ	
27	Preaching of the gospel; light	
28	Eternal life	
29	Departure	
30	Blood of Christ; begin life purpose	
31	God; Great Shepherd; offspring	
32	Covenant	
33	Promise	

NUMBER	Positive Meanings	Negative Meanings
34	Naming of a son	
35	Hope	
36		Enemy
37	37 multiplied by 3 equals 111 (My Beloved Son / first born); word of God; energy	
38		Slavery
39		Disease
40	Completed rule; generation; probation; completion of a particular span of time appointed by the Spirit	Trials; testing;
40K	Extraordinary ability to wage wise warfare	
42		Israel's oppression
44	Judgment of the world	Judgment of the world
45	Preservation	
50	Freedom; jubilee; Great Spirit; Pentecost; relates to life purpose (5=serve, 10=accept or reject) acceptable service or not	
50K	Incredible fire of testing	
60		Pride; measure of our image; usually has a negative meaning
66		Idol worship
70	Completely accepted (depending on context); universality	Years of captivity; completely rejected (depending on context)
73	Unformed matter	
90	The fruit has been inspected	
100	Fully begun; children of promise; chosen	
111	My Beloved Son; first born	
119	Spiritual perfection; victory	
120	End of flesh	
133	Unity	
137	God of Gods; chlorophyll (life of plants); creation	
144K	Those numbered with God	
153	Kingdom multiplication; joint heirs; Sons of God	
200	Fully judged	Fully judged
300	Fully conformed	
496	Perfect; blood	
555	Triple grace	
666	Fullness of creation; fullness of reconciliation of all things in heaven & earth	Full lawlessness
792	Salvation; Jesus Christ	

NUMBER	Positive Meanings	Negative Meanings
888	Resurrection; Jesus; tree of life; Holy Spirit	
1000	Maturity (4=rule; 4000 mature rule)	
1500	Authority; light; power; divine completeness; YHVH	
4000	Salvation	
6000		Deception
7000	Final judgment	Final judgment
144K	Those numbered with God	

HEBREW ALEPHBET WITH NUMERICAL VALUES

" I am the God your father, the God of Abraham, the God of Isaac, and the God of Jacob."

Exodus 3: 6

Hebrew Alephbet with Numerical Values

The Hebrew Alephbet consists of twenty-two letters. Each letter has a meaning as well as a numerical value. For example, the Word *El* uses two letters, *Aleph* and *Lamed*. In the Ancient Hebrew pictograph writing, *aleph* was a pictograph of an Ox, which signifies strength, and *lamed* pictures a shepherd's staff which signifies care and guidance. The two together give us the understanding of the word *El* as meaning "a strong leader who keeps us together on the right path." The numerical value of the word *El* is 31.

Numeric Value	Modern	Name	Ancient	Meaning
1	א	Aleph		Ox or bull head, which denotes strength; leader; power
2	ב	Bet		Tent; house, family, inside
3	ג	Gimmel		Camel; to lift up; pride; foot
4	ד	Dalet		Door; entrance
5	ה	Heh		Man with arms raised; look; reveal; breath; behold
6	ו	Vav		Tent Peg; add; secure; hook

7	ז	Zayin		Mattock or hoe; food; cut or cut off; nourish
8	ח	Het		Wall; outside; divide; inner room
9	ט	Tet		Basket; surround, contain; mud or clay
10	י	Yod		Arm with closed hand; work;
20	כ	Khaf		Open palm, bend; open; allow
30	ל	Lamed		Shepherd's staff; teach; control
40	מ	Mem		Water; chaos; massive
50	נ	Nun		Sprout or fish; continue; heir; life
60	ס	Samekh		Thorn; grab, hate, protect; support; endless cycle
70	ע	Ayin		Eye; watch; know; experience

80	פ	Peh		Mouth; blow; speak; to open
90	צ	Tzadi		Man on his side; a trail; Wait; chase; snare; hunt for insights; fish hook; harvest
100	ק	Kuf		Sun at the horizon; condense; circle; time
200	ר	Resh		Head of a man; first; top; beginning
300	ש	Shin		Two front teeth; sharp; press; eat; two
400	ת	Tav		Crossed sticks; mark; sign; monument; covenant

There are five letters that have a specific form when used as the last letter of a word. Some say that the final letters of Kaf, Mem, Nun, Pei and Tzadei have numerical values of 500, 600, 700, 800 and 900. My studies have revealed that there is no traditional Jewish basis for that interpretation, as these letters were added to the alephbet at a later time. There are countless references on the internet and in books on the study of Gematria, a discipline of Jewish mysticism which teaches in depth on the numerical values of Hebrew letters. The pictographic language gives clearer understanding of the original writings and is further confirmation of the use of pictures in word and/or writing to convey spiritual truth.

PERILS OF SPIRITUAL LANGUAGE

"For ask now the animals and they will teach you; ask the birds of the air and they will tell you. Or speak to the earth, and it will teach you; and the fish of the sea will declare to you. Who is so blind as not to recognize in all these that it is God's hand which does it? In His hand is the life of every living thing and the breath of all mankind."

Job 12:7-10

Perils of Spiritual Language

Know what you mean and mean what you say. Often, people who are spiritual have a hard time explaining what they mean in a way that a person who has no spiritual history or church involvement can understand. Those who are "church goers" have a tendency to get used to speaking with others in their own group, using phrases and/or words those who are outside the group can't understand. Those involved in New Age or other types of faith practice use terms that usually only those familiar with that particular faith practice can understand.

In my experience, trying to use everyday language to explain my own beliefs caused me to realize that I did not have a full understanding of some of the terms I used. This section is simply an explanation of spiritual terms for those who may not understand spiritual language, or for those who would like to be able to explain these terms in every day language.

Some words in this list are specific to the Christian faith and some are considered New Age or some other faith practice. As a lover of God, and follower of Jesus, I offer these definitions from my own perspective and limited understanding. It is my hope that by better understanding each other's language, we will be better equipped to communicate effectively with each other while gaining a better understanding of each other's faith practices. This list is not exhaustive.

Akashic Record - It is believed by many spiritists through history (such as Edgar Cayce) that all thoughts, words, and actions are recorded in a universal filing system, also known as the collective conscience. It is said to contain all knowledge.

Animism - The belief that natural objects have souls that may exist apart from their material bodies.

Anointing – The ritual act of applying oil either by rubbing on or pouring over that which is to be anointed. Moving in *the anointing* is when a person yields to the presence of God so completely that he becomes temporarily as one with Him, consciously allowing God to take control so that His perfect will is accomplished. Signs, wonders, and miracles frequently happen because God, the creator and maintainer of the universe, is in action. It is also understood as the manifestation of

106

spiritual inspiration. Those said to be moving in the *anointing* have special abilities while in that state and lack them when out of it.

Astral Projection - When the conscious mind intentionally leaves the physical body and enters the spiritual or astral body and moves about. (By comparison, an out-of-body experience is involuntary.) During this travel, one is believed to remain connected to the physical body by an umbilical cord-like attachment known as the silver cord. See "Out of Body."

Aura - Sometimes seen as a halo, an aura is an energy field that surrounds individual elements of creation, also called *outshining*. Auras differ from one person to another in terms of size, shape, intensity, and color, but are not only seen on human beings. The size and intensity of a person's aura is proportionate to their level of spirituality. I believe that this is the part of Peter that healed those he passed by, translated in many Bible versions as his *shadow*.

Authority - The right bestowed by God to direct others. True authority is perceived by others, and is not something you have to force upon them. Authority is given by God and made evident by people, circumstances, and results.

Automatic Writing - Writing that is performed without any conscious thought and typically believed to be performed by means of connection with a spiritual source.

Blessing - Something that is very good that you have received, such as a special favor or gift. It infers the idea that what has been received comes from God. Also used to mean the invoking of God's favor upon someone. See "Speak a Blessing."

Body of Christ - This term includes all people who are followers of Jesus, also called Christians. It is also used to refer to members of churches, or Christians in general. It is believed that all those who believe that Jesus is the Messiah collectively make up His body in the earth.

Bondage - This term refers to the problems some suffer in life from which they are unable to get free. This can include fear, depression, other mental problems, as well as physical addiction. It can also refer to spiritual beliefs, such as legalism, that produce fear and dread rather than life.

Book of Life - A book where the name of every person ever born is recorded along with all their thoughts, words, and actions throughout their lives. It is thought that this book may include the Book of Remembrance mentioned in the Bible book of Malachi where even our conversations about God are recorded. A person whose name is blotted out of this book faces eternal death and is not allowed to enter heaven.

Born again - When a person believes that Jesus died on the cross to make a way for them to enter into relationship with God, the Holy Spirit enters their spirit and regenerates their spiritual being. This process of recreation is also called being *born again*. It is the time when a person's true life begins.

Call of God - Once you are born again your perspective on life changes and you see yourself as part of a bigger purpose and you become aware of a certain life purpose (see "Destiny") that you desire to fulfill while you are on the earth. The awareness is sometimes called the *call of God* on your life.

Call on your life - Same as above. Some people seem to have a passion for a particular area of life for most of their lives, and some acquire this passion at a certain time or event. This understanding of your life purpose is also described as being *called* by God or of having a *call on your life*.

Calling - Same as *call on your life*. Whatever it is you have the above described passion for is also known as your calling.

Chakra - The word *chakra* means *circle* or *ball*. It is an energy field that emanates light. According to yoga philosophy, there are seven of these energy centers in the human body that correspond to certain endocrine glands; may give off color that indicates health condition; are said to be the connecting point of soul to body; sometimes called an aura; and their frequencies correlate to the musical scale.

Channeling - The practice whereby a medium enters a trance in order to convey messages that are received from a spirit guide. The medium relinquishes control of their body to be used by a spiritual being and allows the entity to speak through them.

Check in your spirit - This term refers to the times when you have a "feeling" that you can't quite explain but you know for sure that something is not right, or you have a sense that you should proceed with caution.

Clairaudience - The psychic ability to hear things that are outside the normal range of human perception. This is similar to the Christian teaching of hearing *in the Spirit.*

Clairvoyance - The psychic ability to see things that are outside the normal range of human perception. This is similar to the Christian teaching of seeing *in the spirit.* Also known as intuition or spiritual perception.

Cleansing - Many times we make choices, experience things, or have certain ways of thinking that are not good for us. Reaching a point when we feel regret for our actions and want to be free from the feelings of guilt, shame, and/or effects of those experiences or thought processes indicates a desire for *cleansing.* Receiving cleansing may require us to forgive others and ourselves. This is accomplished by expressing our regret and sorrow concerning our behavior and/or thinking to God through prayer, also known as *confessing our sins.* Christian faith teaches that once the confession is made, all is forgiven and cleansing happens instantly. Some faith practices also encourage the use of physical cleansing such as fasting and enemas.

Demons - These are negative spiritual entities that use their influence for the dark side, are part of Satan's kingdom, and possess a deep hatred for God and man. Some people believe they are the fallen angels who left heaven in the Luciferian rebellion.

Destiny - A person's destiny is also known as his or her life purpose. It is predetermined by God and may be a course of events or a single accomplishment that is considered as something beyond human power or control.

Disciple - May refer to a student or to the act of teaching. Typically used to mean the in-depth training of a person in a particular doctrine or spiritual belief, that requires a more involved relationship between teacher and student.

Dowser - This is the name for a person who has the ability to perceive the location of water that is untapped in the earth. This is usually done using a forked shaped stick and is sometimes called *water-witching.*

Dream Catcher - Native American object that looks like a spider web and has different meanings to different tribes. One belief is that it is used to protect dreamers from bad dreams. Negative dreams are ensnared in the web and disappear with sunrise, while the good dreams slip through the hole in the middle and slide down over the attached feathers to the dreamer.

Dream Interpretation – Hebraic method - Dreams are considered as communication from God. An interpreter using the Hebraic method of dream interpretation simply gives voice to the message that God is speaking to the dreamer.

Dream Interpretation – Jungian method - Dreams are considered a message from your own subconscious. The interpreter explains what your inner self is trying to reveal to you about yourself.

Edification - The result of being built up in a spiritual or moral sense and can also mean to be encouraged. Also used to mean enlightenment.

Enemy - Term usually used in reference to dark, negative spiritual forces; or may speak of anyone who is working against you.

ESP - An acronym that stands for the words *extra-sensory perception* and is used to describe the ability to perceive the spirit realm without using the physical senses.

Faith - The ability to take possession of an outcome that is hoped for as if it was already a reality. Sometimes used to mean what you believe in, such as your religious beliefs, and/or what you believe to be true.

Favor - Progress seems easy, as if something or someone was making a way for you; people allow you to go forward in work, etc.

Fruit - Evidence of good things being accomplished in your life

Gaia - Name of the goddess of Earth from Greek mythology. *Gaia* is also used to refer to the belief that everything on and in the earth forms a system that can be considered a single organism. Some use the term Mother Earth as synonymous.

Generational ties or sins - Term used to mean problems and/or issues that are a result of problems and/or issues of your ancestors. It is believed that the sins of those in your bloodline may affect your life physically and/or spiritually.

Gifts - Special abilities that are given to a person by the Great Creator that are not the same as a natural talent.

Grace - Defined as the undeserved favor and love of God, can also mean the influence of the Holy Spirit working in your life, seemingly making things easier to accomplish

Graphology - Study of the systems of writing; also known as the study of someone's handwriting that is said to reveal information about the writer such as character, personality, and/or abilities.

Great Creator - I use this term to refer to the One True Light; the God of Abraham, Isaac, and Jacob who is the creator and sustainer of all that exists. I use this term interchangeably with God, He Who Loves Me Most, and Jesus.

Great Spirit –I use this term interchangeably with Holy Spirit, breath of God and the One True Light as explained above.

Guru - Originally came from Hinduism, means a person who is a mentor, a spiritual leader, or someone who knows a lot about a particular subject. Sometimes used to express that someone is an expert in a given field.

Holiness - God is a spiritually pure or holy being, and *holiness* is used to mean a state of living that imitates Him. Christians believe that it is faith in Jesus that makes it possible to be holy and to be cleansed from the wrong actions or attitudes one has committed. Some Christians use this term to describe their lifestyle (usually meaning their abstaining from what is considered sin).

Judgment - This term, when used in reference to judgment coming from God, means a particular misfortune or event that is the consequence of sin. It is believed that judgment from God can often be avoided when those who are being judged show their desire to change their behavior or attitudes.

Justification - This term, when used by followers of Jesus, means an act of God that makes a person "just as if they had never sinned," and is used to explain what was accomplished by Jesus dying on the cross for the sins of mankind. It is believed that faith in that work erases all sin whether past, present, or future, and makes it possible for humans to enter into the presence of a Holy God while alive on the earth and enter heaven upon physical death.

Kabala - Term used for the ancient tradition of mystical Judaism. It refers to teachings that were once considered secret, that are said to give deeper understanding of God and the intricate workings of creation.

Karma - This term is used by those who believe in reincarnation to mean that things done in another life cause a debt that must be paid in this life. If bad things happen, it is believed it is because of your having done something bad that you are being paid back for in this life. In current common use, it is akin to the meaning of the saying *what goes around comes around*. It is similar to the Christian teaching of *what you sow you will reap*.

Kirlian Photography - A method used to photograph auras.

Lamb's Book of Life - When someone is born again, his or her name is written in the *Lamb's Book of Life*. It is referred to when people speak of someone arriving at the gate of heaven and having the gatekeeper check to see if his or her name is in the book before allowing entrance.

Leading, or to feel led - This term is used to describe the intuitive sense of direction sometimes received from God. Usually it is connected to a feeling or a sense that you are to do a particular thing or go a particular way.

Mantle - This simply means the authority and/or anointing in which a person operates. See "Authority" and/or "Anointing."

Mantra - A common word or phrase that is repeated while in a state of meditation or prayer; it originally comes from a Hindu practice of chanting a verbal formula repeatedly.

Metaphysics - A branch of philosophy that examines the nature of reality; it is also known to mean the science of things beyond the physical dimension.

Ministry - Whatever is done for the benefit of others. For example, encouraging a friend who is having a hard time may be referred to as your having ministered to your friend. It can also be a reference to a life purpose, or acting on a passion based on something you sense God is asking you to do. See "Call of God."

Nirvana - Most often used to mean a place or state of existence that is heaven-like. The term comes from beliefs in Hinduism and Buddhism, but is often used in common speech to mean having attained complete bliss or joy.

Numerology - Study of the occult meaning of numbers and their influence upon an individual. It is based upon numerical values such as a person's date of birth, letters in their names, etc. Numerology does not require psychic ability.

Occult - The literal definition is that which is mysterious, what is beyond the ordinary range of knowledge, or that which is hidden from view. The term is also used to describe practices using magic, astrology, or any system that claims to tap into knowledge of secret supernatural powers. It is typically used by Christians to mean something negative or having to do with dark forces.

Open Heaven - Term used to mean that you are enjoying a time where it seems that your prayers are answered right away and everything in your life seems to be blessed by God. See "Blessing."

Out of Body - Refers to an experience where one has the sensation of being outside one's own body and sometimes results in perception of things that could not otherwise be known. The experience is generally believed to be involuntary (such as a near-death experience), although some use the term to mean the experience of astral projection, which is voluntary.

Palmistry - This is a popular method of giving readings that involves foretelling of one's future through the study of the lines, shapes, wrinkles, and curves on the palm. Palmistry does not require psychic ability.

Pantheism - Typically is believed to mean the belief in many different gods, it also means the belief that God is the universe and not a personal Being.

Paradigm - Your way of viewing reality is based on certain values, beliefs, assumptions, etc., and constitutes a model that is the structure of your thinking. Your *paradigm* is the lens through which you view the world.

Paradigm Shift - A fundamental change in your beliefs or way of doing things.

Paranormal - Outside the normal range of experience and scientific explanation. It is usually understood to mean an occurrence in connection with ESP, or supernatural phenomenon.

Parapsychology - Study of events or phenomenon that cannot be explained with natural means; specifically study of ESP, telepathy, clairvoyance, etc.

Poltergeist - Literally means *noisy ghost*. This term is sometimes used to refer to a demon, as a poltergeist is known to make rapping sounds or other noises in order to create fear and/or disorder.

Praise - Term used for the expression of your feelings about God to God. Praise can be spoken directly to Him or stated about Him such as "You are worthy!" or "Glory to you, Lord, for you are righteous and just, perfect in all your ways!" Praise is sometimes expressed through song.

Prayer - Prayer is simply conversation or dialogue with God. It is sometimes used to mean the making of a request to God and can also mean the recitation of a written, specially worded request.

Precognition - Term used to describe the ability to know something in advance which is usually attributed to ESP or clairvoyance but may also be prophecy.

Prophecy - Same as above. Used to mean the foretelling of what is to come by receiving information from God. Also used as a general description of revelatory speech. Term is also used in regards to those of the Christian faith who speak for God.

Prophesy - To speak a word of prophecy.

Prophetic - This term is used to classify the different abilities having to do with revelatory gifting.

Purity - Quality of being free from contaminants; for followers of Jesus, the term is used to mean living a life that is righteous and abstaining from actions or attitudes that are contrary to the teachings of scripture.

Reading - Psychic - A psychic reading is given by a person who is considered a psychic and is generally offered to give direction for the future.

Reading - Spiritual - A spiritual reading given by a Christian is done by asking God for a prophetic word for the one desiring the reading. It may be done by an individual but is usually done by a team of three who give the reading to one person. It is intended to provide encouragement, comfort, and edification. It may or may not include the foretelling of any events.

Reap what you sow - The consequences of your actions have been realized. What you give your time and energy to will become evident in your life. It is a spiritual law that what you measure out to others will be measured back to you, for example, if you are unwilling to show mercy to someone, a time will come when you will desire to be shown mercy but it will not be available for you. The term karma is often used in our current culture as synonymous; however, it has a different meaning. See "Karma".

Recompense - To pay back with something that is equivalent to what was received or taken; to compensate or to make amends by something that is equal in value.

Redemption - To buy back something; pay a ransom; used by followers of Jesus to describe Jesus' act of paying for deliverance and forgiveness of sin by giving himself to die on the cross.

Reincarnation - The belief in the rebirth of the soul in one or more successive lives.

Repent - To make the decision to change for the better as the result of remorse or regret regarding one's behavior, attitudes, and beliefs. It is said that true repentance is when we decide to agree with God about our lives and destiny.

Repentant heart - The realization that your actions, attitudes, and/or lifestyle are not pleasing to God, resulting in a desire to change those and turn toward God.

Resurrect - Something or someone dead comes back to life.

Revelation - Refers to a supernatural disclosure or bringing to light that which had previously been hidden; usually understood to come from God.

Ritual - A particular procedure that is followed for a religious or other type of rite; usually a ceremonial set of actions that result in a particular outcome.

Sanctification - The process by which someone or something is made pure, and/or holy.

Satan - The Hebrew word for *adversary*; the chief of the fallen angels, formerly known as Lucifer, and believed to be the prince of darkness; also called the devil.

Saved - Christian term that means to have believed that Jesus' death on the cross provides a way to be forgiven and begin a new spiritual life; term is used interchangeably with born again.

Séance - A meeting held for the purpose of contacting the dead; usually includes a spiritist who acts as the medium through which the dead spirits speak.

Self-realization - Term used to mean the knowledge gained through life experience, as opposed to book learning whereby you gain knowledge of your true self.

Shaman - Term refers to a person that has special spiritual abilities and is used interchangeably with *witch doctor*. A shaman acts as a medium between the invisible and visible worlds and is usually part of a tribal society. They perform rituals for healing, to control nature, or for knowing the future.

Sin - A fault or offense. An act of disobedience to God's law. Can also refer to wrongdoing, whether in thought or action.

Speak a blessing - To speak of good things to come for a person, family, city, etc. There is power in the spoken word, so to speak out those things that you desire to see released or those things that you believe are going to be released actually enables them to come.

Spirit Guide - Typically used to define a spirit being whose purpose is to protect and offer instruction to guide a person through their life decisions. Christians have a similar teaching concerning guardian angels.

Spiritual food - Refers to spiritual teaching that when heard, actually refreshes you and is said to feed your spiritual man.

Spiritual gifts - Special abilities that are given to a person by God; may be given before birth, during childhood, or as an adult; these are not the same as natural abilities or talents, but usually encompass some type of spiritual ability such as knowing things about people, knowing the future, seeing spiritual beings, etc.

Stronghold - Refers to beliefs that people hold as true in their lives that in actuality are not true. For example, if someone has been told all his life that he is no good and will never amount to anything, the defeatist attitude he develops is actually a *stronghold* in his thinking.

Strongman - Refers to a demon that holds a certain territory. It is said to have great power and be the strongest of the group of demons with which it is associated.

Synergy - The result of the cooperative interaction of two or more people or groups. It is believed that by the act of cooperation, the result is much greater than could be achieved by the individual. Typically this refers to the combination of spiritual energies, not physical effort.

Tarot Cards - Usually used to mean the 22 cards of a 78 playing card deck. The tarot cards are pictorial cards that are used in fortunetelling.

Telekinesis - Literally means *distance movement* and refers to the ability to move objects using only the power of the mind.

Telepathy - Commonly used to mean the ability to read someone's mind. It can also mean the ability to perceive information without the use of the five physical senses.

Thanksgiving - The act of expressing your feelings of being thankful.

Third Eye - Term used to describe the ability to see into the spirit realm. It is believed to be connected with the pineal gland, which is located between the two hemispheres of the brain.

UFO - An acronym for *unidentified flying objects*; usually associated with a belief in alien life.

Vision - This term is used to mean a spiritual experience whereby an image is seen either with the mind's eye, or the actual physical eyes. Most often this is attributed to receiving information from God.

Visualization - Used to mean a mental picture as with use of imagination or daydreaming. The practice is said to be beneficial in building up faith and hope, by *seeing* what you are expecting before it manifests in the natural realm.

Washed with the Blood - This phrase refers to the spiritual act of believing that Jesus' blood was shed for your sins. This belief is pictured by being immersed in Jesus' blood as if in a bath with the result being all your sins are washed away.

Wilderness - A time when things are not very clear and you may feel that you cannot seem to find the answers you are seeking.

Wisdom - The ability to discern what is right and true. Sometimes used to mean the ability to know what to do with the knowledge you have obtained.

Witchcraft - The term is used today to describe the practice of Wicca religion, the pagan nature religion. Sometimes used as synonymous with the worship of Satan, but witchcraft and Satan worship are actually two distinct religious practices. It is sometimes understood to mean the practice of black arts.

Word from God - Term used to mean receiving instruction from God; may come in the form of a feeling, someone speaking to you, reading, or seeing something in nature.

Word of God - Usually refers to the book called the Bible, or Holy Scriptures. Also known as the Ancient Writings.

Types of Dreams

"For God does reveal His will; and speaks not only once, but more than once, even though men do not regard it. One may hear God's voice in a dream, in a vision of the night, when deep sleep falls on men, while slumbering upon their beds."

Job 33: 14- 15

Different Types of Dreams

There are several different methods used to interpret dreams. You may have a dream interpreted by different people and find that they come up with entirely different interpretations. This is usually because they are using different methods to arrive at their interpretation.

The method I advocate is called the Hebraic method, simply because it follows the pattern of the interpretations used in the Ancient Writings of Scripture. It is my belief that not all dreams are to be interpreted, because dreaming is a natural phenomenon. That fact tells me that there are dreams that occur which are not messages from God, but may be induced by any number of other factors. The important thing is to learn the difference.

While I do not wish to elaborate on the different methods, I do want to make you aware of different types of dreams that you may experience so that you have an idea of which dreams should be given your attention and which types you can safely disregard.

The following information is not exhaustive, but should give you an idea of the types of dreams you may experience and help in learning how to distinguish the differences.

You may want to make a practice of noting in your dream journal what type of dreams you have. For example, if you awaken realizing that you had a physically induced dream due to illness, just note in your journal the date, the fact that you were ill, and that you had a body dream. You may also want to note if it was chaotic, scary, etc.

It is interesting to note that in concert with the lunar phases and your hormonal cycle, you may begin to note a pattern in how dreams are presented. This will also help you to distinguish your dreams and realize the particular time when you are most likely to receive a "message" dream from God. God works in times and seasons, so don't think it strange that you could actually learn the pattern and participate with God in it.

Different Types of Dreams

Body Dreams are caused by the state of your physical body. If you are sick, on medication or having a particularly hard time in a stage of your hormonal cycle, your dreams may be very strange and troubling.

Calling Dreams reveal what you are supposed to do with your life. They give you understanding of a direction you should go in. They also help you to fulfill your destiny in the earth. An example of a calling dream would be one where you see yourself teaching, helping others, and/or following a particular path. Generally the information in a calling dream will be confirmation of something you have already been shown or felt; they are not usually of something that you have never even considered.

Chemical Dreams are a result of using drugs and/or alcohol because those components usually interfere with your ability to enter a state of restful sleep, thus your R.E.M. sleep may be agitated causing nightmares or bizarre dreams that can be troubling. Prescription or over the counter medications can have the same negative effect upon your dreams.

Cleansing Dreams facilitate the cleansing process of spiritual purification and usually contain some component of relief. This may include a scene where you are using a toilet, taking a shower, or removing something from your body.

Correction Dreams give you some type of corrective information. They reveal to you how to behave in a given situation and cause you to realize that prior to this you have been behaving in the wrong way. If from God they will leave you with understanding and peace and will not make you feel condemned, though feeling a need for repentance would be an appropriate response to a God given correction dream.

Deliverance Dreams are given to allow for actual deliverance from oppression in a person's life. These may contain a component of relief and can include taking something off your body, vomiting, coughing, screaming, or some other action that leaves you feeling as though you are lighter, freer, and/or different. You will be aware of the change upon awaking.

Direction Dreams give you information on how to make a decision. They usually give you very specific instruction and may include clear understanding of what will be the result.

<u>Encouragement Dreams</u> simply leaves you with a feeling that you can make it. They are given to encourage your heart and give you hope.

<u>False Dreams</u> present information that is not true as though it were true. They usually contradict something that you have already been shown or understand to be from God. These can be generated from the enemy or may come from the struggles within your own soul.

<u>Fear Dreams</u> reveal to us things that have been given power in our own lives. They are given for the purpose of revealing information to us so that we can then get rid of the fear.

<u>Healing Dreams</u> bring forgiveness and love. Example: a deceased loved one appears and you are able to express things you did not get to say before he or she passed. This brings you relief and healing of heart.

<u>Intercession Dreams</u> cause us to pray for someone else or for a distant problem. These dreams can be used to show a person that he is to intercede on behalf of a person or situation and may reveal some specific information that can be used in those prayers.

<u>Invention Dreams</u> offer ideas for new inventions. Sometimes the solution to a problem with a prototype will be revealed in this type of dream. There are many examples given in history where this is true, among them are the sewing machine, ideas for new business, scientific discoveries, etc.

<u>Prophecy/Revelation Dreams</u> reveal to you something that you could not have known in the natural. They give you understanding in certain circumstances or give information that is specific. They may contain information on a future event or give clarity concerning what is happening currently.

<u>Revealing of Self Dreams</u> are given to reveal something about you to yourself. If you are feeling a certain way in a situation but have stuffed your feelings, you may receive a dream that simply reveals your heart. These dreams also can be God showing you an area in your life where your behavior or attitudes are not pleasing to Him and need to be changed. It is usually difficult for us to see our own areas of weakness, so God is gracious to allow us to watch ourselves from an objective perspective so that we can make the necessary changes to enhance our natural and spiritual lives.

Soul Dreams are generated from our soul in response to strong desire of which we may not be aware. These can happen in different ways, such as a woman whose husband has left her for another woman, dreams of reconciliation where the other woman is rejected and the marriage is saved; a person has been deeply wounded by someone in authority over him or her may dream of being vindicated and the abuser being publicly humiliated. Once these dreams are recognized, the issue that is addressed needs to be dealt with by the dreamer so that it has no further power in his or her life.

Spiritual Warfare Dreams usually entail involvement in some type of struggle. You may be fighting a person or an unseen force, you may have some type of weapon, or you may only use your voice. Many times, what is accomplished in the dream is actually accomplished in the spirit realm.

Warning Dreams warn you about something that is to come. They may reveal the enemy's plans so you can change them through prayer. These dreams may let you know of something in your own life that needs to be changed. Example: Dreaming about not taking a particular trip that was planned, taking a different route or mode of travel.

Word of Knowledge Dreams are given to reveal the solution to a problem or, in dealing with a particular issue, the root of the cause. They are given from God and reveal information that you did not know in the natural.

Countries & Their Mottos

"My country 'tis of thee, sweet land of liberty, of thee I sing. Land where my fathers died, land of the pilgrims' pride, from every mountainside, let freedom ring."

AMERICA My country, 'tis of Thee
Lyrics by Samuel F. Smith - 1832

Countries and Their Mottos

When the location of a dream is a foreign country, it is wise to consider what the name of the country means as well as your own feelings about that country. While it may indicate your need to pray for the people of that particular area, or indicate your own desire or calling to go to that place, it may also be a hidden message having to do with what the name of the country means, or the country's motto.

Country	Motto
America	One from many; In God we trust
Andorra	Strength united is stronger
Antigua & Barbuda	Each endeavoring, all achieving
Argentina	In union and freedom
Bahamas	Forward, upward, onward together
Barbados	Pride and industry
Belgium	Unity is strength
Belize	Under the shade I flourish
Brazil	Order and progress
Brunei	Brunei, the abode of peace
Bulgaria	Union is strength
Cambodia	Nation, Religion, King
Canada	And he shall have dominion also from sea to sea
• Alberta	Strong and free
• British Columbia	Splendor without diminishment
• Manitoba	Glorious and free
• New Brunswick	Hope was restored
• Newfoundland & Labrador	Seek ye first the kingdom of God
• Nova Scotia	One defends and the other conquers
• Nunavut	Nunavut our strength - or Our land our strength
• Ontario	Loyal she began, loyal she remains
• Prince Edward Island	The small under the protection of the great

Country	Motto
• Quebec	I remember
• Saskatchewan	From many peoples, strength
Chile	By reason or by strength - or freedom and order
East Timor	Honor, country and people
Fiji	Fear God and honor the Queen
France	Liberty, equality, fraternity (brotherhood)
Germany	Unity and justice and freedom
Greece	Liberty or death
Guyana	One people, one nation, one destiny
Haiti	Unity is strength
India	Truth alone triumphs
Indonesia	Unity is diversity
Iran	God is most great
Kenya	Let's work together
Kiribati	Fear God , respect the King
Laos	Peace, independence, democracy, unity and prosperity
Luxembourg	We want to stay what we are
Malaysia	Unity provides strength
Mauritius	Star and key of the Indian Ocean
Monaco	With God's help
Namibia	Unity, liberty, justice
Nauru	God's will first
Nepal	The motherland is worth more than the kingdom of heaven
Netherlands	I will maintain
Netherlands Antilles	Unified by freedom
North Korea	One is sure to win if he believes in and depends upon the people
Norway	All for Norway
Philippines	For love of God, people, nature and country
Poland	God, honor, homeland
Saint Lucia	The land, the people, the light
San Marino	Liberty
Senegal	One people, one goal, one faith

Country	Motto
Seychelles	The end crowns the work
Sierra Leone	Unity, freedom, justice
Singapore	Onward Singapore
Spain	Further beyond
Andalusia	Andalusia for herself, for Spain and for humanity
Soviet Union	Workers of the world unite
Suriname	Justice, piety, loyalty
Swaziland	For Sweden, with the times
Thailand	Land of smiles
Turkey	Peace at home, peace in the world
Tuvalu	Tuvalu for the Almighty
Ukraine	Freedom, accord, goodness
United Kingdom	God and my right (droit = right hand side)
Scotland	No one injures me with impunity
Wales	Wales for ever
Cayman Islands	He hath founded it upon the seas
Falkland Islands	Desire the right
United States	In God we trust - or - Out of many, one
Uruguay	Liberty or death
Vietnam	Independence, liberty and happiness

United States
Nicknames & Mottos

"...you are no longer outsiders excluded from the rights of citizens; but you now share citizenship with the saints; and you belong to God's own household."

Ephesians 2:19

United States Nicknames and Mottos

State Name	Nickname	State Motto
Alabama	Yellowhammer State	We dare defend our rights
Alaska	Last Frontier	North to the Future
	Land of Midnight Sun	
Arizona	Grand Canyon State	God Enriches
	Copper State	
Arkansas	Natural State	The People Rule
California	Golden State	I Have Found It (Eureka!)
Colorado	Centennial State	Nothing Without Providence
	Colorful Colorado	
Connecticut	Constitution State	He Who Transplanted, Sustains
	The Nutmeg State	
	The Provisions State	
	The Land of Steady Habits	
Delaware	The First State	Liberty and Independence
	The Diamond State	
	The Blue Hen State	
	Small Wonder	
Florida	The Sunshine State	In God We Trust
Georgia	The Peace State	Wisdom, Justice and Moderation
Hawaii	The Aloha State	The Life of the Land is Perpetuated in Righteousness
Idaho	The Gem State	Let it be Perpetual
	The Gem of the Mountains	
Illinois	The Prairie State	State Sovereignty, National Union
Indiana	The Hoosier State	The Crossroads of America
Iowa	The Hawkeye State	Our Liberties We Prize and Our Rights We Will Maintain

State Name	Nickname	State Motto
Kansas	The Sunflower State	To the Stars by Hard Ways
Kentucky	The Bluegrass State	United We Stand, Divided We Fall
Louisiana	The Pelican State	Union, Justice and Confidence
Maine	The Pine Tree State	I Direct
Maryland	The Old Line State	Manly Deeds, Womanly Words
Massachusetts	The Bay State	By the Sword She Seeks Peace Under Liberty
	The Old Colony State	
Michigan	The Wolverine State	If You Seek a Beautiful Peninsula, Look Around You
	The Great Lake State	
Minnesota	The North Star State	The North Star
	Land of 10,000 Lakes	
Mississippi	The Magnolia State	By Virtue and Arms
Missouri	The Show Me State	Let the Good of the People be the Supreme Law
Montana	The Treasure State	Gold and Silver
Nebraska	The Cornhusker State	Equality Before the Law
Nevada	The Silver State	All For Our Country
	The Sage State	
	The Sagebrush State	
New Hampshire	The Granite State	Live Free or Die
New Jersey	The Garden State	Liberty or Prosperity
New Mexico	Land of Enchantment	It Grows as it Goes
New York	The Empire State	Higher
North Carolina	The Old North State	To Be Rather Than to Seem
North Dakota	The Peace Garden State	Liberty and Union, Now and Forever, One and Inseparable

State Name	Nickname	State Motto
	The Flickertail State	
	The Roughrider State	
Ohio	The Buckeye State	With God, All Things are Possible
Oklahoma	The Sooner State	Work Conquers All
Oregon	The Beaver State	She Flies With Her Own Wings
Pennsylvania	The Keystone State	Virtue, Liberty and Independence
Rhode Island	The Ocean State	Hope
	The Plantation State	
South Carolina	The Palmetto State	While I Breathe, I Hope
South Dakota	The Mount Rushmore State	Under God the People Rule
Tennessee	The Volunteer State	Agriculture and Commerce
	The Big Bend State	
	The Hog & Hominy State	
	The Mother of Southwestern Statesmen	
Texas	The Lone Star State	Friendship
Utah	The Beehive State	Industry
Vermont	The Green Mountain State	Freedom and Unity
Virginia	The Old Dominion State	Thus Always to Tyrants
	The Mother State	
Washington	The Evergreen State	By and By
West Virginia	The Mountain State	Mountain Men Are Always Free
Wisconsin	The Badger State	Forward
Wyoming	The Equality State	Equal Rights

JEWISH PRAYERS FOR PREPARATION FOR SLEEP

"A dream not interpreted is like a letter unopened."

Babylonian Talmud Brakhot 55a

Hashkivenu

Lay us down, Adonai our God, in peace,
and raise us up, our Ruler, to life.
Spread over us a sukkah of Your peace
and set us right with good counsel from You.
Save us for the sake of Your Name,
shield us and remove from us
enemies, plague, sword, famine, and woe.
And remove spiritual impediment
from before us and behind us,
and shelter us in the shadow of Your wings.
For You are God who protects and rescues us,
for You are God, the gracious and compassionate Ruler.
Safeguard our going now and forever.
and our coming, for life and peace.

Invocation of Angels

In the Name of Adonai God of Israel:
May Michael be at my right,
Gabriel at my left,
Uriel before me,
and Rafael behind me;
and above my head the Shekinah of God.

Hamapil

Blessed are You, Adonai our God, Ruler of the Universe,
Who casts the bonds of sleep on my eyes
and slumber on my eyelids.
May it be Your Will, Adonai my God and God of my ancestors,
that you lay us down in peace and raise us up to peace.
May my ideas, bad dreams or evil fantasies not trouble me.
May my bed be complete before You,
and may You illuminate my eyes, lest sleep be death.
For You are the illuminator of the pupil of the eye.
Blessed are You, Adonai Who illumines
tho wholo world with Your Glory.

Recommendations for further study:

Numbers in Scripture:

Bonnie Gaunt. *Genesis One.* Kempton, IL: Adventures Unlimited Press, 2003 or any of the other numerous books she has authored.

Del Washburn and Jerry Lucas. *Theomatics, God's Best Kept Secret Revealed.* Briarcliff Manor, NY: Stein and Day, 1977.

E. W. Bullinger. *Number in Scripture, It's Supernatural Design and Spiritual Significance.* Grand Rapids, MI: Kregal Publications, 1967

Ancient Hebrew pictographs:

Dr. Frank T. Seekins. *Hebrew Word Pictures.* Phoenix, AZ: Living Word Pictures, Inc., 2003

Jeff A. Benner. *The Ancient Hebrew Lexicon of the Bible.* College Station, TX: Virtualbookworm.com Publishing Inc., US 2005

MY NOTES

7345976R00083

Made in the USA
San Bernardino, CA
05 January 2014